11/97

DOUGLAS MacARTHUR
AND THE CENTURY OF WAR

DOUGLAS MACARTHUR AND THE CENTURY OF WAR

ROBERT A. SCOTT

Facts On File, Inc.

In memory of
Barbara Boland

Douglas MacArthur and the Century of War

Copyright © 1997 by Robert A. Scott

Facts On File, Inc.
11 Penn Plaza
New York NY 10001

Library of Congress Cataloging-in-Publication Data

Scott, Robert Alan.
    Douglas MacArthur and the century of war / Robert A. Scott.
    p. cm.—(Makers of America)
  Includes bibliographical references and index.
    ISBN 0-8160-3098-7
    1. MacArthur, Douglas, 1880–1964. 2. Generals—United States—Biography. 3. United States. Army—Biography. 4. United States—History, Military—20th century. I. Title. II. Series: Makers of America (Facts on File, Inc.)
  E745.M3S36 1997
  355'.0092—dc21
  [B]   97-6874

You can find Facts On File on the World Wide Web at http://www.factsonfile.com

Text design by Catherine Rincon
Cover design by Matt Galemmo
Illustrations on pages 11, 24, 36, 51, 95 by Dale Wiliams

Printed in the United States of America

MP FOF 10 9 8 7 6 5 4 3 2 1

This book is printed on acid-free paper.

CONTENTS

1

"A NEW ERA IS UPON US"
Tokyo Bay, September 2, 1945

On August 29, 1945, the most powerful armada ever to float pulled into Tokyo Bay. American soldiers swarmed ashore from transport ships and assault landing craft. They seized the ruins of a port city, Yokohama, just to the south of Japan's capital, which was also in ashes. Still wary of their defeated enemies, the Americans deployed in defensive lines around Yokohama and waited to occupy Tokyo itself after a formal surrender. The situation was quiet but tense.

Over the past six months American bombs had turned practically all of Japan's cities into blazing funeral pyres, where hundreds of thousands of men, women, and children perished. But the survivors and the rest of the population living in the relative safety of the countryside got no sign from their country's military government that it might give up the war. Radio broadcasts reviled the Americans as bloodthirsty and heartless, calling on the Japanese people to rise up and fight the expected invasion by the United States and its allies. Most people did not know of the nuclear fireballs the Americans unleashed over the cities of Hiroshima, on August 6, and Nagasaki, on August 9—or of the huge Russian forces that fell upon Japan's mainland Asian empire on August 8 and soon began to move down the Korean peninsula toward Japan itself.

Suddenly, it seemed to most Japanese, their supreme ruler, Emperor Hirohito, broadcast a personal message on August 14,

On the deck of the U.S. battleship, Missouri, *on September 2, 1945, the Japanese delegation waits to surrender.* (MacArthur Memorial Archives)

ordering them to surrender. "One day we were fighting furiously and everybody in the country expected to die on the field of battle," said a young Japanese diplomat, Toshikazu Kase. "The next day, it was over and Japan had lost." Three million Japanese soldiers were waiting to make a final stand on their home soil. No one knew if all would obey the emperor and submit to the fewer than 300,000 American and British troops coming to occupy the country.

But on August 31 reporters with the Americans at Yokohama drove jeeps out through the U.S. lines and headed straight for Tokyo. Armed only with cameras and pens, they were the first Americans to reach the capital. The highest-ranking Japanese official they could find to interview was the young diplomat, Kase, who worked for Foreign Minister Mamoru Shigemitsu. A graduate of Harvard University, Kase was at home with English-speaking reporters. He was asked, one of them wrote, "if he thought Japan would want to make another try at world domination in, say, another fifty years. He looked out his window at the panorama of devastated Tokyo. 'We are paying a very great price for our attempt,' he said. 'However, if your treatment is too severe, the Japanese people will react.'"

It was obvious by then that the harsh terms imposed on Germany after the European disaster of World War I had not prevented the rapid development of an even more powerful and militaristic nation or the onset of a far more devastating and truly global war. As Japan's August 1945 collapse ended World War II, people around the globe wondered how to avoid yet another war among great powers in the future—a war that would be the most catastrophic of all because nuclear weapons now existed. Nations must find ways of settling disputes without destroying each other in the process, commentators reasoned. "In the atomic age it is either one world or no world at all," *Time* magazine declared.

Even amid the devastation, some Japanese saw a chance to address this life-and-death issue. "Can we not," a Tokyo newspaper asked "build up for the first time in the history of mankind a great power without arms?" But Kase feared that a harsh occupation, intended to punish the country and prevent a full recovery from the war, would plant the seeds of future conflict. By September 2, as he joined a gloomy group of 11 Japanese soldiers and diplomats to represent their country at the formal surrender, bitter comments by some powerful Americans seemed to have confirmed Kase's fears.

In the quiet of a gray dawn, the Japanese delegation drove from Tokyo to Yokohama and boarded a U.S. destroyer, the *Landsdowne*. Foreign Minister Shigemitsu, leader of the group, limped awkwardly aboard on his cane and wooden leg. Years before, a would-be assassin had maimed him with a bomb.

Kase wrote that as the ship pulled out of the harbor he could see "line on line of gray warships, both heavy and light, anchored in a majestic array . . . floating like calm sea birds on the waters." It took an hour for the *Landsdowne* to reach a huge battleship, the *Missouri*. Shigemitsu struggled up the steep gangway at the head of his group, lurching back near the top. Hundreds of U.S. sailors in their dress white uniforms brightened the decks. American officers showed the Japanese where to stand, facing a table and a microphone and, just beyond them, admirals and generals of the United States and its allies: China, Great Britain, the Soviet Union, Australia, Canada, France, Holland, and New Zealand.

The victors stared coldly at the Japanese. "A million eyes seemed to beat on us," Kase recalled. ". . . I felt their keenness sink into my body with a sharp physical pain . . . We waited . . . standing in the public gaze like penitent boys awaiting the dreaded schoolmaster."

Finally, two American officers strode onto the deck. One was Admiral William F. Halsey, commander of the fleet that filled Tokyo Bay. In a speech recorded the day before to be broadcast back to the United States, he had hailed "the complete defeat of the treacherous foe." Overly lenient treatment of the vanquished country, he warned, would "sure as death and taxes lead to another war." Thousands of Halsey's sailors were soon to go ashore as part of the occupation force. His boss, U.S. Pacific commander Admiral Chester W. Nimitz, had announced that under "the Navy's administration . . . the Japanese will not be allowed to forget they are defeated and are paying the penalty for their aggression and treachery."

But, although the surrender took place on a navy ship and under the guns of the navy's fleet, the navy was not in charge. Admiral Halsey took his place among the lines of officers from the victorious countries; the army officer with him stepped to the microphone. He had recently been appointed supreme commander of the Allied powers in the Pacific and put in charge of occupying Japan.

He was widely known as one of the most pompous and vain leaders in the American military, a schemer who coveted status and authority, fond of posing as a dashing hero and of wearing elaborate uniforms covered with his medals. But on this day he wore plain, baggy khakis. As he read slowly and emphatically from a sheet of paper, Kase could see the page flutter slightly in General Douglas MacArthur's trembling hand.

> We are gathered here, representatives of the major warring powers, to conclude a solemn agreement whereby peace may be restored. The issues, involving divergent ideals and ideologies, have been determined on the battlefields of the world and hence are not for our discussion or debate. Nor is it for us here to meet, representing as we do a majority of the people of the earth, in a spirit of distrust, malice or hatred. But rather it is for us, both victors and vanquished, to rise to that higher dignity which alone befits the sacred purposes we are about to serve, committing all our people unreservedly to faithful compliance with the understanding they are here formally to assume.
>
> It is my earnest hope, and indeed the hope of all mankind, that from this solemn occasion a better world shall emerge out of the blood and carnage of the past—a world dedicated to the dignity of man and the fulfillment of his most cherished wish for freedom, tolerance and justice.

To Kase, it seemed as if these words "sailed on wings . . . For me, who expected the worst humiliation, this was a complete surprise. I was thrilled beyond words, spellbound, thunderstruck . . . This narrow quarterdeck was now transformed into an altar of peace."

When representatives of Japan and the other countries had stepped forward and signed the surrender document, MacArthur said, "Let us pray that peace be now restored to the world and that God will preserve it always. These proceedings are now closed." As the Japanese left and bomber formations droned overhead in a final show of strength, MacArthur moved to another microphone where, thanks to recent advances in radio, his words were broadcast live to the United States and all over the world. "Today the guns are silent," he began.

> A great tragedy has ended. A great victory has been won. The skies no longer rain death—the seas bear only commerce—men everywhere walk upright in the sunlight. The entire world lies quietly at peace. The holy mission has been completed. And in reporting this to you, the people, I speak for the thousands of silent lips, forever stilled among the jungles and the beaches and in the deep waters of the Pacific which marked the way . . .
>
> A new era is upon us. Even the lesson of victory itself brings with it profound concern, both for our future security and the survival of civilization. The destructiveness of the war potential, through progressive advances in scientific discovery, has in fact now reached a point which revises the traditional concept of war.
>
> Men since the beginning of time have sought peace . . . Military alliances, balance of power, Leagues of Nations all in turn failed, leaving the only path to be by way of the crucible of war. The utter destructiveness of war now blots out this alternative. We have had our last chance. If we do not devise some greater and more equitable system Armageddon will be at our door.

The human spirit and character must grow, he said, to "synchronize with our almost matchless advance in science, art, literature and material and cultural developments of the past two thousand years. It must be of the spirit if we are to save the flesh."

Douglas MacArthur believed that the hope for a human renaissance lay in human freedom. Japan became aggressive, he pointed out, when it turned away from democracy. The scientific knowledge that the country gained from the West "was forged into an instrument of oppression and human enslavement. Freedom of expression, freedom of action, even freedom of thought were denied through the suppression of liberal education, through appeal to superstition, and through the application of force." He vowed to "see that the Japanese people are liberated from this condition of slavery."

From an underground bunker at the imperial palace in Tokyo, Emperor Hirohito listened to the surrender ceremony by radio, then studied a report hurriedly prepared by Kase. "He is," Kase wrote of the general, "a man of light." Rather than return to the passivity and seclusion that he had maintained until his intervention ended the war, Hirohito decided to show his people how he wanted them to deal with the Americans. The emperor, considered by Japanese tradition a divine being who called on no one and who was rarely seen in public, informed the Americans that he would like to visit General MacArthur. This visit was an unmistakable signal to Hirohito's government, military, and people of support for and submission to the American leader. It cleared the way for a historic occupation that built a democracy on the ashes of Imperial Japan.

To some people Douglas MacArthur was indeed a man of light. Many idolized him. Many others loathed him. Over the years scholars have put together a mixed picture. He was a brilliant, complex, and captivating personality, ambitious and driven. He moved from war to government and from government to war in one of the longest and most distinguished careers in the history of either one. He was one of the very first American leaders to appreciate the political power of mass communications. He was a soldier with political aspirations who tried to face down his superior, the president. He was a man with little of a private life whose personal strength contributed to many of his country's victories and whose personal weaknesses helped lead it to disaster.

Yet it takes more than a career study or personality profile of Douglas MacArthur to consider how he matters now. The outline of his life describes the rise of the world's greatest power, the United States, and the historic transformation of war in the 20th century. His obsessions included not only power, glory, and the trappings of authority but the survival of democracy and, through it, of humanity itself. This last issue remains one of the great questions of today. This was what Douglas MacArthur pleaded for in September of 1945 when he had the ear of the world.

At the age of 65 he had reached the highest post of his life, riding at the crest of American power and ideals as they surged to the shores of Asia. They were part of him and he of them almost from the day of his birth.

2

UNDER THE FALCON'S WING
1880–1898

L ate in the spring of 1884 U.S. Army Captain Arthur MacArthur II led about 50 soldiers with a dozen of their wives and children south from the mountains of northern New Mexico into the dry southern section of the territory. In a 400-mile trip of several weeks, they moved down the valley of the Rio Grande and approached New Mexico's boundary with Mexico. The captain had orders to occupy Fort Selden, an abandoned outpost near the river, about 50 miles north of the border.

His wife, Mary, and their two young sons, Arthur III and Douglas, accompanied him. Douglas, the younger of the two boys, had spent most of his four years with his parents in isolated forts of the West. But this new home was particularly remote. It lay deep within the region of desert and dry lands that stretches across the American continent, from the Pacific Ocean and the Gulf of California on the west to the Gulf of Mexico on the east. It includes northern Mexico and the southwestern United States, forming a great natural barrier between North America and Central America.

The 1,000-mile-long Rio Grande and its main tributaries, especially the Conchos flowing north through Mexico, bridged this frontier. Their waters sustained life, and their channels marked a pathway through the desert. The rivers linked native peoples of North America with the more developed and wealthy civilizations that flourished in Central America before the coming of the Europeans in the 16th century. Corn, the first domesticated plant in the Americas, was passed up the Rio Grande system to the mountain valleys of northern New Mexico, where it became the mainstay of the Indians who inhabited pueblos, or adobe (sun-dried brick) villages, in the Southwest.

Mary Hardy MacArthur, Douglas MacArthur's mother, sometime before her marriage in 1875 (MacArthur Memorial Archives)

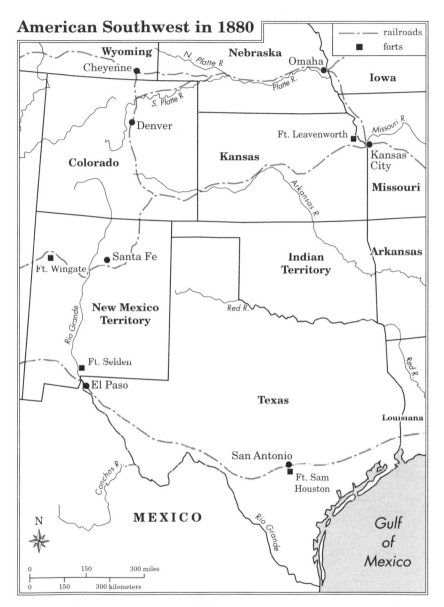

American Southwest in 1880

--- · --- railroads
■ forts

Douglas MacArthur spent his childhood and youth in the American South-west. This map shows the four army posts where he lived.

The river road also brought the Spanish and their horses into North America from Mexico starting in the early 1500s. The Spaniards and their Mexican successors subjugated the pueblos and other local native peoples and stayed until the

American conquest of New Mexico, Arizona, and California in the Mexican-American War of 1846–47. After decades of warfare against the Apaches and other tribes, by 1884 the U.S. Army had broken the power of the Indians throughout the region and confined all but a few to reservations. The first railroad lines spanned the New Mexico Territory. Yet it was still a very thinly settled and wild country. The civilian territorial government could not maintain order. Rival railroad builders competed and even fought for control of vital routes. Cattle barons and their hired gunfighters fought homesteaders for control of land. Thieves and cattle rustlers roamed the country. Outlaws made good use of the international boundary, dodging from one side to the other to thwart pursuit by Mexican or U.S. authorities.

Arthur MacArthur II and his small detachment, Company K of the U.S. 13th Infantry Regiment, went to Fort Selden to guard a nearby crossing of the Rio Grande and the trail along the river and to provide a base in the border country for roving cavalry units. Fort Selden was just a collection of crumbling adobe buildings with dirt floors. But life there "was vivid and exciting for me," Douglas MacArthur recalled years later in his autobiography, *Reminiscences*. "There were the visiting officers and mounted details from the cavalry post at Fort Stanton to the east guarding the nearby Mescalero [Apache] reservation. There were the bumpy rides on the mule drawn water wagon that would make the daily trip to the Rio Grande several miles west of the post. And toward twilight each evening, [there was] the stirring ceremony of retreat, when we would stand at attention as the bugle sounded the lowering of the flag."

The boy learned to see this flag as a symbol of order in the wild world around him. He also learned that his father had fought heroically in horrible battles, led many men to their deaths, and very nearly died himself—all for the sake of this flag. The captain was a hero of the Civil War. Arthur II commanded the 1,000-man 24th Regiment of the Wisconsin Volunteers. He survived serious wounds and ended the war a colonel. Throughout his childhood Douglas heard stories of his father's battles. He learned that only a third of the men who served in Arthur II's regiment survived the war. He saw how his father revered them and was in turn revered by the men he had led.

Arthur MacArthur II, Douglas's father, as a newly commissioned lieutenant in the Union Army, 1861 (MacArthur Memorial Archives)

When the Civil War ended in 1865 Arthur II's father, a prominent judge in Wisconsin, urged his son to pursue a career in law. Instead the young man accepted the lowest officer's rank, second lieutenant, to get a place in the country's small postwar army. Over the next two decades he advanced only to the rank of captain and spent most of his time in charge of small infantry units that guarded railroad building crews in the West. He also served in Louisiana during the mid-1870s and met Mary there. They married in 1875. The couple had three sons: Arthur III in 1876, Malcolm in 1878, and Douglas, born January 26, 1880 in a barracks at Fort Leavenworth, in Arkansas.

In 1877 Arthur II went to Pennsylvania to help control the massive rioting that broke out in industrial and mining centers that year. But for the most part his duty was routine and uneventful. On each assignment he served under the direct supervision of a commanding officer and so had little opportunity to continue the leadership he had shown in the war. He did not socialize much with other officers and left most of the child rearing to his wife. He devoured books on history and on political, military, and economic developments around the world. But when the family moved to Fort Selden in 1884 Arthur II, at age 38, was once again the officer in command at his post, however small.

Douglas worshiped his father from afar, for the most part. His mother kept the youngest child close to her. Mary Hardy MacArthur—who went by the nickname Pinky—was 31 years old when she arrived at Fort Selden. The daughter of a prosperous cotton merchant in Norfolk, Virginia, she grew up at Riveredge, her father's estate overlooking the beautiful Elizabeth River. She was a refined and educated southerner. Her brothers had fought for the Confederacy, and some of them strongly disapproved of her alliance with a Union soldier.

Strong-willed and ambitious, Pinky had high hopes for her husband's career and groomed her children to follow his path. Life at isolated army outposts, where Pinky lived in shacks and had to defer meekly to the wives of higher-ranking officers, caused her great frustration but never dampened her ambition. The impression she made on one young child was recorded by Eleanor P. Cushman, who grew up near Fort Selden and years later wrote to Douglas:

I remember her distinctly.

She was like a young falcon. She was vivid, with a glancing quickness of movement. Her eyes were keen and soft at the same time. In my picture of her there is a lot of white muslin dress swishing around, and a blaze of white New Mexican sunlight, and in the midst of it this slender vital creature that I have never forgotten. I was looking at her from somewhere near the floor—my natural habitat at that time—and my picture is exactly like modern photography—and the angle and the light emphasized her swift poise and the imperious way she held her head.

Douglas became his mother's central focus from his early childhood until her death in 1935. One of the likely reasons for this was Malcolm's death from measles 10 months before the family moved to Fort Selden. A second reason was Pinky's decision, having seen her own mother's health wrecked by more than a decade of nearly continuous childbearing, to stop having children.

Though she was grief stricken and tired of frontier life, Mary considered Fort Selden to be an improvement. "It is a lonely place," she wrote a relative in May 1884, "but Arthur is in command and I can do just as I want. I have only three rooms and a small kitchen, but it is enough with my family."

Mary took most of the responsibility for the education of Arthur III and Douglas, as there was no school at the fort. "Our teaching included not only the simple rudiments, but above all else, a sense of obligation," Douglas recalled. "We were to do what was right no matter what the personal sacrifice might be. Our country was always to come first. Two things we must never do: never lie, never tattle." As he grew up Mary made it clear to Douglas that competing and winning was an obligation he owed not only to his country but personally to her. When he was 20, she wrote him this poem:

> Do you know that your soul is of my soul such a part
> That you seem to be fiber and core of my heart?
> None other can pain me as you, son, can do;
> None other can please me or praise me as you.
> Remember the world will be quick with its blame
> If shadow or shame should ever darken your name.
> Like mother, like son, is saying so true

The world will judge largely of mother by you.
Be this then your task, if task it shall be
To force this proud world to do homage to me.
Be sure it will say, when its verdict you've won
She reaps as she sowed: "This man is her son!"

She taught him to revere and follow the example of his father, the commander of what Douglas later called the "lonely garrison" at Fort Selden. The boy saw his father not only as the heroic soldier but as the very seat of order and security in the wild and endless territory around the fort.

"He knew the badmen of those days—the James boys, the Youngers—and the picturesque scouts and lawmen such as "Wild Bill" Hickok and "Buffalo Bill," Douglas wrote. "He was at the center of the disorder, the violence, the fighting involved in this drama of undisciplined and untamed men . . . the savage turbulence, the striking vitality, and the raucous glamour of the struggle for law and order" in the West.

Douglas watched as his father imposed a strict routine of daily drill and ceremony, interspersed with work, inspections and target practice. Arthur II had seen enough fighting to believe deeply in group discipline and preparedness. He kept his distance from the officers and soldiers under him and was demanding as well. But the captain also believed that morale was essential to make a group of men into a cohesive force. He cited men for achievements as well as shortcomings and urged them to compete with other army units in their markmanship scores. He provided the troops with recreation space, where they were allowed to buy beer and tobacco and to shoot pool. He used profits from this canteen to buy better food for the troops. Desertion at Fort Selden dropped to well below that of similar posts, and Arthur II's superiors noticed.

In September 1885, a year and a half after he had taken over the fort, Captain MacArthur received a visit from Major G. H. Burton of the army's western headquarters staff at Fort Leavenworth. The major wrote in his report:

> Captain MacArthur's company was inspected and drilled in full dress, and, subsequently, ordered into camp. The military bearing and appearance of the troops were very fine. Captain MacArthur impresses me as an officer of more than ordinary ability, and very zealous in the per-

Douglas MacArthur (left) in 1884, when he was four years old, with his brother Arthur III at Fort Selden (MacArthur Memorial Archives)

formance of duty. The company and post show evidence of intelligent, judicious and masterly supervision. This company has more comforts in the barracks and amusement room than any other organization I have visited.

A year later the army decided to close Fort Selden. An officer at Fort Leavenworth needed a model company of infantry for a new training school there, and he sent for Company K.

Leavenworth, the army's headquarters in the West for more than 50 years, was a dramatic change for six-year-old Douglas. Here imposing brick buildings enclosed large parade grounds, where hundreds of troops marched, trained, and drilled. Here the army had thousands of men and stockpiles of provisions, weapons, and ammunition, and a large prison. Here officers and their families lived in relatively comfortable wood-frame houses, and the army ran a school for children at the fort.

"It was a never ending thrill for me to watch the mounted troops drill and the artillery fire on the practice range," Douglas later wrote. ". . . There was extra excitement when my father commanded the afternoon parade, with the cavalry on their splendid mounts, the artillery with their long-barreled guns and caissons [ammunition wagons], and the infantry with its blaze of glittering bayonets."

The boy dreamed of becoming a soldier and a leader, but he did not connect this ambition to the new and tedious experience of school. The carefree life of the West, he wrote, "was still in my blood and I was a poor student." Once, when Arthur II was sent off on an expedition, "I begged to go along. But my father just pointed to my report card, saying I needed the schooling."

Douglas's schoolwork improved some after 1889, when Arthur II won promotion to the rank of major and an assignment to the army's legal and records section in Washington, D.C. Nine-year-old Douglas moved to the city with his family. His mother dressed him impeccably in tweed suits and enrolled him in a public grade school. "Washington was different from anything I had ever known" he wrote. "It was my first glimpse at that whirlpool of glitter and pomp" in the national capital. He remained, Douglas added, "only an average student."

But Douglas's appreciation of books and learning did grow as he got to know his grandfather. The Scottish-born Judge Arthur MacArthur was 72 in 1889. He had practiced law in Milwaukee during the 1840s and 1850s and then gone on to the bench, first as an elected judge in Wisconsin and then, in 1870, as an appointee of President Ulysses Grant to the federal court of appeals serving the capital district. The judge's influence had won Arthur II an officer's commission in the 24th

Wisconsin Volunteers in 1862 and helped bring him the assignment in Washington in 1889.

The judge and his third wife, Mary, lived in a handsome home, tended by servants; he had an imposing library and many impressive friends. In the years immediately after his retirement he was also a prolific writer on a variety of subjects.

Judge Arthur MacArthur, Douglas's grandfather (MacArthur Memorial Archives)

└—Through personal contact and through his books Judge Mac-Arthur had lasting influence on his son and grandsons. It was through him, Douglas wrote, that the American MacArthurs had descended from a "warrior clan," the MacArtairs of Scotland, whose traditions "are linked with the heroic lore of King Arthur and the Knights of the Round Table." It was most likely from the judge that Douglas heard the clan's battle song of vigilance and preparedness:

> MacArtair, Most High, where the wild myrtles glisten,
> Come, buckle your sword belt and Listen! O Listen!

The judge enlarged on the sense of duty and mission that Douglas absorbed from Arthur II. The eldest MacArthur believed, as he wrote in one of his books, that the worldwide conquests of the British Empire were the result of the inborn vitality and aggressiveness of the Anglo-Saxon, "who is certainly the most unique and wonderful specimen of the race that has yet appeared in history." In the American West, Judge MacArthur wrote, the Anglo-Saxons of the United States "soon established their supremacy, developing the resources of this great region, and prepared it for the order and freedom of our institutions" while displacing the Spanish and French who, though the judge considered them to be among the "civilized races," were still inferior to the Anglo-Saxons.

The judge believed that the Anglo-Saxons were the world's pioneers of self-government, law, and liberty. It was their destiny to rule most of the world and to pass their traditions and even their language on to the rest of humanity. The Celtic people of Scotland had, he wrote, likewise "been selected as an instrument in civilization of the world." Both Arthur II and Douglas would show commitment to these principles later in their lives.

Douglas spent considerable time with his grandfather. "I could listen to his anecdotes for hours," he wrote. ". . . It was he who taught me to play cards and, incidentally, the game of poker."

Arthur III's example was also an important influence on his brother. The older boy did well in school and in 1892 won a coveted appointment to the U.S. Naval Academy at Annapolis.

Soon the younger son had his own opportunity to put on the uniform of a military school. He wrote:

> In September 1893, my father was ordered to Texas. I hailed this move with delight. Housing the largest garrison I had ever seen, Fort Sam Houston guarded our southern borders and was one of the most important posts in the Army. It was here that a transformation began to take place in my development. I was enrolled in the West Texas Military Academy . . . My studies enveloped me, my marks went higher . . . My four years there were without doubt the happiest of my life."

In August 1896, Judge MacArthur died. He had spent the last months of his life convincing influential friends to write letters of support for Douglas's application to enter West Point in 1897. The grandson remembered: "The last [poker] hand I ever played with him I held four queens and in my elation bet every chip I had. I can still feel the shock when he laid down four kings. And I have never forgotten his words, 'My dear boy, nothing is sure in this life. Everything is relative.'"

Douglas soon saw how true this advice was. Though he graduated at the top of his class in the spring of 1897, he did not get the West Point appointment. That year Arthur II was assigned to St. Paul, Minnesota. Douglas and Pinky moved to the judge's original home base of Milwaukee to establish residency there and try to get Douglas an appointment to West Point through the local congressman. The congressman announced that whoever earned the highest score on a competitive examination in the spring of 1898 would be his choice. To prepare, Douglas went to classes at a Milwaukee school and worked privately with a tutor and with his mother, studying math, science, and history. He wrote:

> I never worked harder in my life . . . The night before the examination, for the first time in my life I could not sleep, and the next morning . . . I felt nauseated. But the cool words of my mother brought me around. "Doug," she said, "you'll win if you don't lose your nerve. You must believe in yourself, my son, or no one else will believe in you. Be self-confident, self-reliant, and even if you don't make it, you will know you have done your best. Now, go to it."

When the marks were counted, I led. My careful preparation had repaid me. It was a lesson I never forgot. Preparedness is the key to success and victory.

STUDENTS OF WAR
1898–1903

By the time Douglas MacArthur learned that he had won a place at West Point, his desire to attend had vanished. In the spring of 1898 the United States went to war against Spain. His brother, who was by then a junior navy officer, and his father, who moved into the upper ranks of the army with a promotion to general, got ready for action. They left Douglas at home with his mother to get ready for school. He had more than a year to wait before entering the academy and then four more years of study. The 18-year-old pleaded for permission to enlist in the army immediately, but his parents would not allow it. "There will be plenty of fighting in the coming years," his father said. "Prepare yourself."

All Douglas could do was follow newspaper reports and seethe in Milwaukee as he watched the adulation showered on other young men because they were in uniform. He no longer lived at a fort. He was not even a student-soldier. He was an idle civilian. But the Spanish-American War was a crucial turning point in his life. Not only did it raise his father to national prominence, it fundamentally changed the mission of the army that Douglas would serve for the next 50 years. That army's job had been to guard the borders of the country and maintain security in the western territories taken from the Indians. In 1898 the United States began sending large numbers of soldiers and sailors to fight in faraway lands.

The United States' Possessions and Dependencies

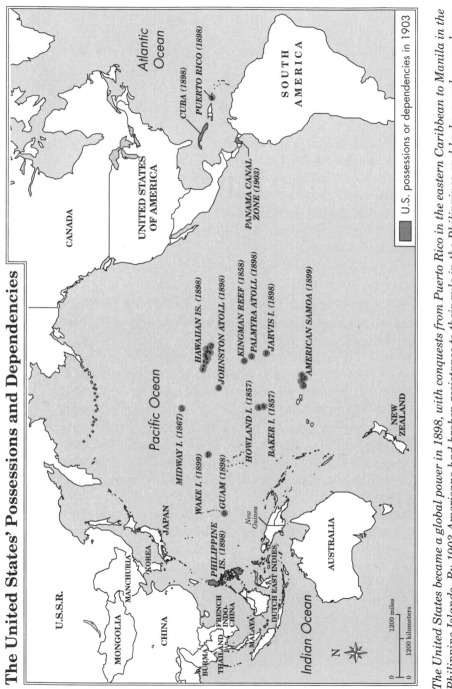

CANADA

UNITED STATES
OF AMERICA

*Atlantic
Ocean*

CUBA (1898)

PUERTO RICO (1898)

SOUTH
AMERICA

PANAMA CANAL
ZONE (1903)

U.S.S.R.

MONGOLIA

MANCHURIA

KOREA

JAPAN

CHINA

Pacific Ocean

MIDWAY I. (1867)

HAWAIIAN IS. (1898)

JOHNSTON ATOLL (1898)

KINGMAN REEF (1858)

PALMYRA ATOLL (1898)

JARVIS I. (1898)

AMERICAN SAMOA (1899)

WAKE I. (1899)

GUAM (1898)

HOWLAND I. (1857)

BAKER I. (1857)

PHILIPPINE
IS. (1898)

New
Guinea

BURMA

THAILAND

FRENCH
INDO-
CHINA

MALAYA

DUTCH EAST INDIES

AUSTRALIA

NEW
ZEALAND

*Indian
Ocean*

N

0   1200 miles

0   1200 kilometers

☐ U.S. possessions or dependencies in 1903

The United States became a global power in 1898, with conquests from Puerto Rico in the eastern Caribbean to Manila in the Philippine Islands. By 1903 Americans had broken resistance to their rule in the Philippines and had secured a canal zone across the Isthmus of Panama. The canal opened in 1914, greatly increasing the reach and power of the U.S. Navy.

The war began with a dispute over Spain's repressive government in Cuba and the mysterious explosion and sinking of the U.S. battleship *Maine* after it anchored in Havana's harbor to demonstrate American concern. Weeks before declaring war in late April 1898, the United States had planned the first action it would take: an attack in the Philippines, the huge chain of tropical islands in the western Pacific, half a world away from Cuba.

On May 1 a squadron of American ships under Commodore George Dewey sank a Spanish fleet in the sheltered waters of Manila Bay near the port of Manila, the capital and trading center of the islands. Twelve days later and about 10,000 miles away, other American ships bombarded the Spanish at San Juan, Puerto Rico. In the following months the United States claimed an empire stretching almost 10,000 miles between these two port cities. Douglas's brother saw action on a U.S. gunboat in Cuban waters. Their father was one of the leaders of American troops sent to the Philippines.

The United States seized Puerto Rico and Cuba from Spain and annexed the formerly independent Hawaiian Islands in the mid-Pacific Ocean. It also took a string of possessions leading from Hawaii across the vast Pacific almost to Asia. These included: Wake Island, a scrap of previously unclaimed land; the Spanish island of Guam; and Manila. Finally, in 1898 the United States adopted the goal of building a canal across the isthmus of Central America, which would allow the navy to move forces relatively quickly between the Atlantic and the Pacific Oceans.

The country not only acquired Spanish colonies, in the case of the Philippines it inherited the Spanish position of colonial master. Puerto Rico became U.S. soil in 1917, and its people became U.S. citizens. Cuba was occupied for about three years and then became what was called in diplomatic language a "protectorate" of the United States. Officially the island was an independent country, but the United States claimed the right to intervene in its affairs at will.

The Filipinos got neither citizenship nor any pretense of independence. They had struggled against Spanish rule for centuries. When Dewey struck at Manila Bay the Filipinos rebelled once again and overthrew the colonial government almost everywhere in the islands except for Manila, where the

Spanish were trapped between rebels on land and Dewey's ships in the bay. When Americans under Arthur MacArthur II and another general landed and prepared to take the city, Filipino rebels welcomed them as allies. The Spanish yielded the city to the U.S. forces on August 13. The next morning, the Filipino soldiers surrounding Manila were appalled to see American troops facing them from the positions the Spanish had held the day before. The rebels had thrown out one foreign ruler—Spain—only to face invasion and subjugation by a new one: the United States.

By the time Douglas MacArthur entered West Point, in June 1899, Spain had signed the Philippines over to the United States under the terms of a peace treaty. Savage fighting had broken out between the Americans, whose principal combat commander was Arthur II, and the Filipinos. A heated controversy had begun within the United States over the morality of waging of a war against Filipino independence. Reports on the fighting were front-page news. Arthur II was approaching the pinnacle of his career. In 1900 he would become the army's top commander in the Philippines and the first American governor general of the islands.

Every cadet and every teacher at the academy knew who Arthur MacArthur II was, and his son was singled out for special attention. West Point's upperclassmen hazed Douglas unmercifully that summer. One night he submitted to a series of humiliating calisthenics until his muscles ached, and then was wrapped in heavy blankets and put into a steam bath. He fainted, and classmates carried him to a tent, where he went into convulsions. His legs beat on the wooden floor. Another cadet said later that MacArthur "finally asked me to throw a blanket under them in order that the company officers could not hear his feet striking the floor." If the officers had learned of his condition, he might have been discharged from the academy.

Months later, during investigations by Congress and the army into hazing, MacArthur upheld academy tradition, and his mother's order never to tattle, when he refused to identify his tormentors. His steadfast composure under hazing and under examination earned him the respect of classmates. It was just one of the ways in which he emerged at West Point as a leader's leader. He worked relentlessly and ranked at the top of his class; indeed, he had one of the best records of any cadet in academy history. For the rest of his life, MacArthur identified very strongly with the institution where he achieved such success. He loved the image of "the long gray line" of academy graduates stretching through the years, watching over American democracy, ever faithful to their motto: "Duty, Honor, Country."

Douglas MacArthur's success was so important to Pinky MacArthur that even the chance to live in a palace and help her husband as he ruled the Philippines could not lure her to Manila. Instead she lived at a hotel next to West Point. Academy rules, designed to isolate students in a nearly monastic environment of drill and study, forbade cadets to leave the grounds. But Douglas regularly sneaked to the hotel to report to Pinky.

Besides the endless drilling and marching, inspection and weapons training, he studied history—especially the history of war—math, science, and engineering. Though not a particularly gifted athlete, MacArthur participated avidly in sports. Cadet MacArthur was tall (an inch under six feet), dignified, and handsome. He had an extraordinary memory that enabled him to repeat facts, figures, and large blocks of text years after one quick reading.

In one science course MacArthur and the other cadets struggled with a complicated concept of atomic physics. "The text," he wrote later, "was complex and, being unable to comprehend it, I committed the pages to memory. When I was called upon to recite, I solemnly reeled off almost word for word what the book said. Our instructor, Colonel Feiberger, looked at me somewhat quizzically and asked, 'Do you understand this theory?' It was a bad moment for me, but I did not hesitate in replying, 'No, sir.' You could have heard a pin drop. I braced myself and waited. And then [came] the slow words of the professor, 'Neither do I, Mr. MacArthur.'"

Douglas followed reports of the fighting in the Philippines closely and was awed when his father became governor general. He told a roommate he "wanted to be a worthy successor" to Arthur II. Talking with a sergeant on the academy staff who became his friend, "he often wondered if he could ever become as great as his father, and he told me that if hard work had anything to do with it, he had a chance."

The father's example, and the son's aspirations, went far beyond combat tactics and leadership. When he was appointed governor general in May 1900 it became Arthur II's job to implement American rule over millions of people in the Philippines at a time when the United States was deeply divided over the purpose and the very morality of that rule. In the months just before this appointment, the administration of President William McKinley clarified its position in the face of bitter dissent at home and mounting casualties in the war.

Leaders on different sides of the issue all but accused each other of treason. A policy of conquest, war critics charged, betrayed the Declaration of Independence, the very words that brought the United States of America into existence. Did the Declaration not state that government exists with the consent of the governed? Did the inalienable rights of humanity not apply to Filipinos? Did the Declaration and the Bill of Rights of the U.S. Constitution stay behind at the water's edge when the flag moved overseas?

From the floor of the U.S. Senate, member Albert J. Beveridge of Indiana answered in January of 1900 that the God-given rights referred to in the Declaration did not apply to Filipinos. The war critics, far from upholding national principles, were betraying American soldiers in battle by giving comfort and encouragement to their enemy, he charged.

Filipinos, according to the senator, belonged to an inferior racial group he called the Malays. Beveridge described them as "a barbarous race . . . dull and stupid . . . incurably indolent . . . like children . . . They are not a self-governing race." White Americans, on the other hand, bore God's blessing as "His chosen people, henceforth to lead in the regeneration of the world," the senator claimed. "The Declaration applies only to people capable of self-government. How dare any man prostitute this expression of the very elect of self-governing peoples to a race of Malay children of barbarism . . . if you deny it to the Indian at home, how dare you grant it to the Malay abroad?"

While referring to the lives of Filipinos as "trifling," Beveridge extolled the wealth of their islands in rice, coffee, sugar, coconuts, hemp, tobacco, bananas, timber, gold, coal, and copper. The people were too lazy and undependable to supply the labor investors would need to exploit these opportunities, he said. But with the help of workers shipped in from outside the Philippines, "young men with the right moral fiber and a little capital can make fortunes there as planters."

The month after this speech McKinley's War Department formally took a similar position concerning the rights of Filipinos. A legal opinion asserted that constitutional rights of U.S. citizens, such as the right to trial by jury, were "part and parcel of our civilization and racial inheritance" and did not apply to "the varied races of the Philippines." The United States remained committed to the idea that the powers of a government "are derived from the consent of the governed," the opinion held, but in the case of the Philippines that consent could be "presumed from the fact of residence in the country."

In May Arthur MacArthur II moved into the magnificent Malacanan Palace on the north bank of the Pasig River in Manila, which had been the home of the Spanish governors,

General Arthur MacArthur II (seated at center) with members of his staff in Manila. The general's experiences in the Philippines, where he became military commander and the first U.S. governor general in 1900, had tremendous impact on Douglas. (MacArthur Memorial Archives)

and began his efforts to implement the policy of conquest. He inherited a force of some 74,000, scattered among more than 500 posts throughout the islands, controlling cities, larger towns, ports, and railroad lines. The Filipino independence forces were poorly equipped but outnumbered the Americans. They controlled much of the countryside and enjoyed the support of most of the population. The Filipinos waged a tenacious guerrilla struggle, hitting the Americans with sabotage, sneak attacks, and booby traps.

As military commander, Arthur MacArthur II sought to crush resistance, while as governor he worked to reward submission. He authorized imprisonment of Filipinos merely on suspicion of collaboration with the guerrillas or for refusal to swear loyalty to the United States. The prisoners would be held until the end of the war, he decreed, except that one would be released in exchange for each gun surrendered. He ordered his soldiers to strike out from their posts in search of guerrilla bands and to burn any villages where they encountered resistance. Filipino soldiers captured in uniform would be imprisoned; those out of uniform would hang.

"My purpose," Arthur MacArthur would later explain, "was to conduct operations in the field relentlessly—with a drastic hand . . . and, on the other hand, in the civil administration to conciliate, to instruct."

Wherever his forces were able to stamp out guerrilla activity the governor general set up local governments and invited Filipino participation in efforts to improve sanitation, vaccinate people against smallpox and other diseases, and provide schools and courts. He repeatedly ordered his commanders to punish soldiers for abuse of prisoners or civilians. He halted reprisals like land confiscation against Filipinos who supported the rebels. MacArthur even published a pamphlet on the U.S. Constitution and promised to respect the civil rights of people in areas where resistance ended.

He refused to recognize the position of his superiors in the War Department that such rights did not apply to "the varied races of the Philippines." Nor would he cooperate with powerful figures in the McKinley administration who thought, like Beveridge, that the Philippines could be exploited with little or no regard for the welfare of the inhabitants. MacArthur thwarted proposals to sell lands cheaply to American investors and to bring in Chinese laborers to work plantations. He advocated allowing Filipinos time to get involved in their government and help shape its development policies. He thought the Filipinos would be able to run the country largely by themselves, though still as subjects of the United States, within a few years.

MacArthur's conciliatory policies had the greatest impact on wealthier, more educated Filipinos who had the time and the ability to get involved in government. But his willingness to promote the basic ideal of human rights in the Philippines put him at odds with official policy. His ideas were not free of a sense of Anglo-Saxon superiority, but MacArthur firmly believed that the desire for freedom and the ability for self-government were universal human traits—not the exclusive attributes of any group or groups.

The United States was justified in conquering the Philippines because it had overriding military and economic reasons for doing so, MacArthur held. The islands offered an ideal position for the basing of naval power off the coast of Asia, whose markets he believed were essential for the growing American economy. But, as he later argued in testimony before Congress, the United States had another, equally vital mission: to "plant firmly and deeply the best type of republican institutions" in the islands ". . . in behalf of human freedom throughout the world."

Thus, while MacArthur embraced his soldier's mission of conquest, he acted on his own ideas of how to rule the conquered.

The war had shown signs of tapering off somewhat by March 1901, when the Americans scored a breakthrough. Emilio Aguinaldo, the leader of Filipino resistance, was captured in a daring raid in the mountains of northern Luzon, the largest and most populated of the islands. MacArthur, ignoring suggestions that Aguinaldo be hanged or imprisoned, brought him as a guest to Malacanan Palace. Eventually he persuaded the Filipino leader to pledge allegiance to the United States, partly by agreeing to release thousands of prisoners. The fighting died down markedly, though guerrillas in some parts of Luzon and elsewhere would not give up.

Many in the United States, and in the government, were outraged by what they considered to be soft treatment of

Filipinos generally and of Aguinaldo in particular. In spring 1901, Douglas felt the sting of this disapproval when the academy's baseball team traveled to the Naval Academy at Annapolis, Maryland, for a game. It was an overcast day, and the navy midshipmen in the stands carried raincoats. They were ready for outfielder Douglas MacArthur when the cadets took the field. He wrote: "I shall never forget the blast that razzed me . . . Every raincoat was swinging, every navy voice joining the ribald ditty:

> "Are you the Governor General or a hobo?
> Who is the boss of this show?
> Is it you or Emilio Aguinaldo?"

On July 4, 1901, Arthur MacArthur II turned the palace and the governor general's job over to a lawyer and politician from Ohio, William Howard Taft. Another officer took over as military commander under Taft's authority, and MacArthur sailed for home.

Taft, like McKinley, gave lip service to the idea that Filipinos should have the benefits of Anglo-Saxon civilization and eventually the right of self-government. But his views were actually close to those of Beveridge. He wrote that it would take the Filipinos 50 to 100 years to get ready for self-government. He spoke of "inferior races" and privately ridiculed MacArthur's regard for Filipinos.

Once the general was gone the most drastic pacification measures begun under his command were intensified and applied widely, sometimes indiscriminately. Whole provinces and the entire island of Samar were laid waste. Food, shelter, tools, work animals, men, and boys were systematically destroyed, and tens of thousands of people left to the mercy of famine. When a small band of guerrillas invaded a peaceful province in southern Luzon, the American governor there reported, the army responded by setting fire to villages and torturing and killing the innocent inhabitants.

Reports of this reached the United States, embarrassed Taft and inflamed controversy over the war. But Taft's close ally, Theodore Roosevelt, succeeded to the presidency when McKinley was assassinated in the fall of 1901. Taft rose within the administration, eventually becoming secretary of war. Early in

1902, when controversy over U.S. conduct of the war led to a congressional investigation, Arthur MacArthur continued his resistance to Taft.

In testimony before a Senate committee the general argued for a concept of universal human rights. The American flag, he said, is "the symbol of human liberty . . . We must regard ourselves simply as the custodians of imperishable ideas held in trust for the general benefit of mankind . . .

"We are now living in a heroic age of human history," Mac-Arthur said, in which Filipinos and Americans will plant "republican institutions and the principles of personal liberty throughout Asia . . . in behalf of the unity of the race and the brotherhood of man . . . Inspiration and hope go with our flag." MacArthur even referred to Filipinos as "a chosen people," using the same terms Beveridge applied to the Americans and British.

Some of the senators' questions reveal just how foreign these ideas were to them. One asked:

> Do you mean that there is among the intelligent Filipinos an intelligent appreciation of our institutions—an understanding?
> MacArthur: I would like to be understood there that it is a realization of an ideal of their own.
> The senator: They have an ideal?
> MacArthur: They have, most decidedly.

Another senator asked, "General, how do you compare the Filipinos with the negro (sic), or is there any comparison between them?"

"I have never made that comparison, Senator," he answered. ". . . To say that they are better or worse than others, I am not willing to go into that . . ."

MacArthur charged that American and European business interests in Manila were pushing for "unrestricted Chinese immigration for the purpose of quick and effective exploitation of the islands; a policy which would . . . be ruinous to the Filipino people."

The next year, in June 1903, the MacArthurs had the pleasure of watching Douglas graduate from the academy at the top of his class. The dignitaries sitting on the speakers' platform

Lieutenant Douglas MacArthur in 1903, soon after his graduation from West Point (MacArthur Memorial Archives)

included all the top-ranked officers present—except for the number three man in the entire army: Arthur MacArthur II. He was relegated to the audience. This was an obvious snub, but even then the extent of the administration's displeasure was not clear to the family. In fact, the general's career was all but over. He nevertheless clung to his beliefs and spent the last years of his life urging them upon his youngest son.

4

"THE WOUND IN MY HEART"
1903–1912

Douglas MacArthur followed his father's path across the Pacific Ocean to the Philippines in the fall of 1903, just a few months after graduating from West Point. The tropical islands, he later wrote, "fastened me with a grip that has never relaxed." By then organized resistance to the United States had collapsed. Among the small group of prosperous Filipinos who before had been allies of the Spanish, many had begun to cooperate with the United States in local and provincial government. This U.S.-sponsored administration under the new governor, William Howard Taft, adopted such forms of democracy as elections. But the poor, the overwhelming majority of the population, were in practice barred from organizing and from holding office. Violence remained commonplace. Gangs operated in the crowded streets of Manila. Generations of conflict between wealthy landowners and their poor tenants continued in farming areas. In some remote regions groups that had contested Spanish rule for many years, including the Muslim Moros, remained outside the control of the Americans.

MacArthur began his career as an army engineer. He traveled to outposts in the islands to help design and build harbors and military camps. On the small island of Guimaras, where he led a squad into the jungle to cut timber for a dock, the young officer came under fire for the first time in his life. Two men, either renegade guerrillas or bandits, tried to ambush him

The Philippines, during World War II

0   100   200 Miles
0   100   200 Kilometers

N

Lingayen Gulf
Luzon I.
South China Sea
Quezon City
Bataan Peninsula
Corregidor I.
Mindoro I.
Calamian Islands
Panay I.
Cuyo Islands
Guimaras I.
Negros I.
Palawan I.
Sulu Sea
N. BORNEO
Sulu Archipelago
Samar I.
Leyte I.
Bohol I.
Mindanao I.
Philippine Sea

MONGOLIA   MANCHURIA
KOREA
CHINA
JAPAN
BURMA
THAI-LAND   FRENCH INDO-CHINA
PHILIPPINES
South China Sea
MALAYA
Pacific Ocean
N
DUTCH EAST INDIES
PAPUA
0   1000 Miles
0   1000 Kilometers
AUSTRALIA

Douglas MacArthur began work in the Philippines in 1903. For the rest of his life this area of the world would hold great importance for him.

when he wandered away from his men to search for timber. A bullet just missed Douglas's head before he killed the men with his pistol. He was unshaken. This would not be the last time that seemingly amazing luck helped him escape death.

In March 1904 MacArthur transferred to Manila, where he was an aide in the army's engineering headquarters. Most of his work involved land surveys for planning of army posts. He toured and mapped the mountainous, jungle-covered peninsula of Bataan, at the mouth of Manila Bay on the northern side. Douglas enjoyed life in this exotic tropical city, with the dazzling sunsets over Manila Bay. Settlement had long since spread beyond the walls of Intramuros, or Old Manila, the fortified town that the Spanish built back in the late 1500s. The city was much as it had been in 1899, when a young soldier named William G. Compton described it in a letter to friends:

> Old Manilla . . . is surrounded by a high stone wall [30 feet high, 10 to 20 feet thick] . . . Running under the walls entirely around the city are dungeons built by the Spaniards in which they put their prisoners . . . going within the walls one sees nothing but low stone buildings . . . The streets of the old city are very narrow and a narrow stone walk runs along each side . . .

As the son of the famous former governor general who had spared Aguinaldo's life, Douglas attracted considerable attention from Filipinos. Among those he met were two young men just out of law school, Emanuel Quezon and Sergio Osmeña. Like Douglas, they were to play major roles in the history of the Philippines.

Malaria brought an early end to MacArthur's first tour in the islands. He fell ill and was sent home late in 1904. A year later, after several engineering assignments in California, he made the long trip by ship across the Pacific Ocean again. This time he landed in Japan and began an apprenticeship under his father that, Douglas later wrote, "was without doubt the most important factor of preparation in my entire life."

Japan, a rising power in Asia, went to war with Russia in 1904. General Arthur MacArthur had long believed in the importance of Asia and the Pacific region to the United States. He had tired of the routine assignments that he received after leaving the Philippines and sought permission to go to Asia and observe the fighting. Early in 1905 the new U.S. secretary of war, William Howard Taft, readily agreed to send his troublesome general overseas. Arthur and Pinky had just reached Tokyo in March when the Japanese defeated the Russians in Manchuria, a huge province in northeastern China lying between Russia and Korea. In May, while the Japanese hosted MacArthur on visits to the battlefields in China, their navy finished the Russians off in the battle of Tsushima Strait, between Japan and Korea. The general got back to Tokyo in September, as Taft arrived to consult with the victorious Japanese.

Taft met with MacArthur and, for reasons he did not explain, asked him to cancel plans for a return visit to the Philippines. In return he offered MacArthur the chance to remain in Asia and to travel widely, visiting military installations of countries throughout the region. Douglas, said Taft, could join his parents as the general's aide.

Lieutenant MacArthur, now 25 years old, reached Tokyo in November. Over the next nine months he and his parents traveled 20,000 miles in southern Asia and in the Malay Archipelago, the thousands of islands that separate the Indian and Pacific Oceans between Australia and the Asian mainland. The MacArthurs eagerly learned all they could about this teeming region—a world the European powers had dominated for the last 400 years, where the native inhabitants lived in what Douglas referred to as a "slave world."

The two great island chains of the Malay Archipelago form the outline of a blossom lying on its side in the tropical seas. The petals open toward the coast of Asia and converge toward New Guinea, which would be the flower's stem. The myriad islands—from tiny spits of coral to islands the size of France with vast, mountainous interiors—form the largest group of islands in the world. And, true to the image of a flower, they support some of the world's most abundant and varied plant and animal life in their rain forests, jungles, mountains, and in the surrounding waters.

European explorers called the islands of the southwestern chain the Malay Barrier because they form a wall between the oceans; the long, narrow islands lie end to end, with narrow straits separating them. The Malay Peninsula, the longest peninsula in the world, is part of this barrier. It reaches more than 1,000 miles from the mainland to within 40 miles of the first island, Sumatra. The other petal of the flower is the Philippines. This chain is somewhat more scattered and more isolated than the barrier islands, separated from the mainland by hundreds of miles. The huge island of Borneo and the octupus-shaped Celebes lie in the blossom's throat, where the two chains of islands converge.

Beginning with the Portuguese in the early 1500s, European powers had built colonial empires to exploit the riches of the Malay Archipelago and the Asian mainland. By the time the United States replaced Spain in the Philippines, Britain, France, Germany, Russia, and Japan as well as the United States were all contending for position in China. The British and Dutch shared control of the Malay Barrier islands. Rubber and fruit had joined coffee and spice in the plantation enterprises of the imperial powers. France moved onto the Asian mainland in Indochina. On the northern side of China, Russia moved into Manchuria.

The Japanese had tried at first to isolate themselves from the encroaching Western powers, much as China tried to do. When they saw China's fate, Japanese leaders decided to follow the example of Britain. Like that island nation, they set out to protect their own shores and to draw power from the conquest of an overseas empire. In 1894 and 1895 they fought and won a bloody war with China. They occupied the island of Taiwan and forced the Chinese to withdraw from Korea.

The rise of Japan came at the same time as the rise of the United States in the Pacific. An ambitious ship-building program, along with completion of the Panama Canal in 1914, were to make the United States a global military power, capable of dominating the Atlantic and the Pacific Oceans. But in the meantime Japan defeated Russia in 1905, the first time that an Asian power humbled a European one. The Americans served as mediators in the negotiation of a peace treaty. Taft, on reaching Tokyo that year, assured the Japanese that the United States recognized their right to subjugate Korea. The Japanese in turn recognized American control of the Philippines. Relations between the two powers were, for the time being, friendly.

Late that year Douglas MacArthur and his parents began the journey that took them through the Malay Archipelago (except for the Philippines) and the European possessions on the mainland. They traveled from some of Asia's largest cities to the most remote outposts of British India in the Himalayan Mountains. They saw China, Saigon in French Indochina, the bristling British fortifications and naval base on the island of Singapore at the tip of the Malay Peninsula, the island of Java and the dozen army and navy bases the Dutch had there, the independent kingdom of what is today Thailand, and the huge British territories of Burma and India.

Douglas spent every day with his parents, and he was with his father most of their waking hours. They bought all the books that they could find on the places they visited, reading and talking through the long hours of travel by ship, riverboat, and train. Douglas had the chance to hear in great detail the story of his father's work in the Philippines and his father's belief in the importance of Asia to the United States.

They lived in embassies, hotels, and guest mansions of the powers whose territories they visited and were treated almost as if the general were a president or king. Douglas remembered:

> We sat in the charmed circles of the chancelleries of the strong and the weak. Kings and viceroys and high commissioners lay bare their hopes and fears . . . We saw the strength and weakness of the colonial system, how it brought law and order, but failed to develop the masses along the essential lines of education and political economy. We rubbed elbows with millions of the underprivileged who knew nothing of the difference between the systems of the free world and the slave world . . .
>
> Here lived almost half the population of the world, with probably more than half of the raw products to sustain future generations. Here was western civilization's last earth frontier. It was crystal clear to me that the future and, indeed, the very existence of America, were irrevocably entwined with Asia and its island outposts.

In the summer of 1906 Douglas returned to the United States with his parents. He was ordered to Washington and placed in the army's prestigious advanced engineer training program. He was also assigned as an aide on the White House staff of

President Theodore Roosevelt, where Douglas's duties were primarily ceremonial. His father, who by then was the second-highest-ranking officer in the army, was, according to tradition, next in line for appointment as commander of the army. Serving even briefly in this post prior to retirement was an honor that Arthur MacArthur II looked forward to.

It was not to be. In January 1907, after the position had become vacant, War Secretary Taft broke precedent by getting Roosevelt to pass over General MacArthur. To the general, a proud man who had served the army faithfully on bloody battlefields and through years of isolation at frontier outposts, the traditions of seniority and rank were sacred. But Taft left him at his post in California as commander of the army's Department of the Pacific, taking orders from an army commander of lower rank.

This was unbearable for General MacArthur. In the spring of 1907 he asked for and received Taft's permission to move back to his home in Milwaukee as an officer without a command. Officially he was there as a consultant, ready to draw on his knowledge and experience for any project or study the army might request of him. But the army ignored him. Arthur became so embittered that he told Pinky not to bury him in his uniform when he died. He left instructions that there be no military display of any kind at his funeral.

His father's humiliation and bitterness were very hard on Douglas. He saw his father as one of the greatest men ever, a brave soldier betrayed by scheming politicians. Soon Douglas's behavior became lethargic, and his own situation began to deteriorate. The commander of the engineering school in Washington wrote that he showed "little professional zeal" for his work. In August 1907 Douglas transferred to an army engineering office in Milwaukee that handled work on harbors and channels in the Great Lakes area. Here he witnessed his father's idleness and got deeper into trouble.

Douglas's superior officer noticed a lack of "a zeal to learn." He showed little interest in his work, the commanding officer wrote, and complained at length when ordered out of the city to work on a major project.

Besides his concern for his father, Douglas found another source of keen personal distress in Milwaukee. He became infatuated with a young woman there, Fanniebelle Stuart. She was apparently from a well-to-do family, for in the space of a few months she lived in Milwaukee, New York City, and Paris. In a series of poems written to Fan in early 1908, Douglas professed his love for her while also warning her of his commitment to the military and portraying himself as a dashing and noble officer worthy of her undying devotion. In one of the poems Douglas's image of himself is a storybook version of his father's experience in the Civil War, except that in the poem the hero dies in battle.

In his fantasy life with Fan, Douglas tells his doting wife as he prepares for battle,

> "My own love! My precious—I feel I am strong
> I exult in the thought of opposing the wrong . . ."

As much as he loves her and their small children Arthur, Malcolm, and Bella, the soldier explains, a foreign invader is closing in on their beautiful valley and he must fight,

> "For home, and for children, for freedom for bread
> For the house of our God,—for the graves of our dead—
> For the leave to exist on the soil of our birth,—
> For everything manhood holds dearest on earth."

Ever dutiful and understanding, she replies,

> "I grudge you not, Douglas—die rather than yield,
> And, like the old heroes, come home on your shield."

He is mortally wounded leading a charge.

In a note with this poem, MacArthur wrote that he was giving her "this peep at my probable destiny" knowing that it would likely ruin his slim chance with her but "in the interest of fair play" so that Fan could see "what might be your lot if you should ever decide to don the army blue." He made clear in another poem that his leaving the army uniform for the sake of a different life with her was out of the question.

> There is a fixed and moveless nature,
> 'Gainst which the tide of passion and desire
> Breaks useless as the water o'er the rock;
> And the warm glow of feeling burns alone
> On the soul's surface, leaving all beneath it
> Unmoved and cold . . .

MacArthur knew full well that the sort of rifle and bayonet battle he described for Fan was no longer a reality. He had read his father's reports on the Russo-Japanese War, where the machine gun demonstrated its ability to mow down waves of attacking infantry. Douglas also knew that Wisconsin was not a likely future battleground. But the poems do reflect his belief in the gallantry of the soldier and the meaning of his sacrifice in shaping the destiny of a nation. He clung to this belief through his life, but with growing foreboding as he saw war change and expand to the point of consuming the very things that his poetic soldier fought for.

Douglas wrote a farewell to Fan in the spring of 1908 as he transferred to his birthplace, Fort Leavenworth. He told her in a note that he expected, wrongly as it turned out, to return in a year to the Philippines. "This means for me," he wrote "the whirling swing of the old life unless some day out there in the jungle a Moro bolo [machete] or a snubnosed forty-five changes it all—into still waters and silence."

At Leavenworth MacArthur took command of a company of engineers—men whose responsibilities included building pontoon bridges, fortifications, and gun emplacements and clearing roads for troops on the move. Taking over a unit with poor morale and performance, he soon demonstrated his ability as a leader. He praised their strengths and pleaded for improvement in weak areas. MacArthur motivated his men to train rigorously, and eventually they became the top-rated unit at the fort. "MacArthur leads—he does not drive," General George Kenney, who worked for MacArthur later, wrote: "People who work for him drive themselves . . ."

One of the men from that group later wrote his former commander:

> As 1st Lt. Douglas MacArthur at Fort Leavenworth, Ks. on the muddy banks of the Missouri you are a definite spot on my memory. You were very proud of your Company K, Third Battalion Engineers . . . You had a nice little outfit in those small days . . . [I remember you] taking the first sergeant's report and about facing to give yours, building pontoon bridges . . . [and joining the men in] races [and] pole vaulting.

Over the next few years MacArthur's performance at Leavenworth overcame the bad reviews he had received in 1907 and earned him more responsibilities. He became an expert in blowing up bridges and other structures and designed training procedures for this dangerous work. In 1911 he was promoted to captain and became head of the engineering department at Leavenworth's field engineering school. Early the next year he was sent to Latin America for two months to observe one of the world's most impressive engineering and construction projects: the building of the Panama Canal.

Back in Milwaukee General Arthur MacArthur formally retired from the army in 1909, and he never wore his uniform again. He was a popular figure in the city, where he had many lifelong friends and was active in veterans' affairs. He was sought after as a public speaker by many groups. Some people even hoped to see him run for governor. But the general preferred quiet days in his library with occasional visits from his sons and grandchildren. Arthur III, Douglas's older brother, was by then on the staff of the Naval Academy and had started a family.

Though he would have nothing further to do with the army, the retired general remained especially devoted to his friends in the dwindling ranks of the old Wisconsin Volunteers. On September 5, 1912, a hot and humid day, he went to the annual reunion of his regiment, 50 years after it had marched off to war. Taking the podium, he began to recall the regiment's harrowing experiences during Sherman's march through Georgia, dangers overcome only with the greatest in teamwork and coolness by soldiers under pressure. "Your indomitable courage," their leader said, and then he faltered. "Comrades," he gasped, "I am too weak to continue."

Arthur MacArthur II collapsed into a chair, then slumped to the floor. His men prayed and draped him with their tattered regimental flag as he died.

His ideals, successes, and humiliation became the lifelong inspiration, ambition, and anguish of his son. Douglas would continue to harbor a deep sense of bitterness and suspicion toward the government he served. "Never," he wrote near the end of his own life, "have I been able to heal the wound in my heart."

5

LORD OF THE CITIZEN SOLDIERS: 1912–1919

Major George S. Patton, an impetuous and promising young cavalry man, stood several miles behind the front lines in northern France in September 1918, during World War I, chatting with another officer. Patton believed in the potential of armored machines to transform warfare. But his lumbering, breakdown-prone tanks were not much use in this war. It was the growing strength of American infantry that was finally starting to push back the Germans. From miles away German artillery fired shells deep into the French and American lines. Occasionally enemy biplanes buzzed overhead, scouting or dropping small bombs. The troops, having pulled back to rest, kept to the relative safety of trenches and dugouts.

The two officers were not in the habit of showing fear. Patton recalled, "We stood and talked but neither was much interested in what the other said as we could not get our minds off the shells." His companion remembered seeing Patton flinch slightly at the sound of an explosion. "Don't worry, Major," Douglas MacArthur said according to his own account, "You never hear the one that gets you."

MacArthur, who at age 38 was one of the youngest generals in the army, seemed utterly heedless of his own safety. In his neatly tailored uniform and polished knee-length boots, he led troops across the most ghastly battlefields the world had ever

By the time Douglas MacArthur arrived in Europe with the Rainbow Division in 1917, World War I had unleashed an unprecedented level of firepower, as this view from the western front near the Somme River in France shows. When the Rainbow joined an offensive the next year in the area of Verdun, an officer with MacArthur described a similar scene: "Craters fifteen feet deep and as wide across, yawned on all sides. All around was a dreary waste of woods, once thick with stately trees and luxuriant undergrowth, but now a mere graveyard of broken limbs and splintered stumps." (Imperial War Museum)

seen. He did not wear a helmet because "it hurt my head" or carry a gas mask because it "hampered my movements." Somehow he survived, his only scar being firsthand knowledge of just how lethal war had become.

Europe's leaders had plunged their peoples into a conflict of unprecedented savagery in August 1914. Lines of trenches and barbed wire now stretched many hundreds of miles between armies on three different fronts. The Germans faced the Russians to the east and the French and British to the west. Germany's ally, Austria-Hungary, confronted Italy to the south. For three long years to the east and south, and four years to the west, the great powers poured out their resources and sacrificed the lives of their soldiers. The British tried to break the will of German civilians with a naval blockade that shut off food imports. The Germans attempted to do the same to Britain with submarines.

The first to collapse was czarist Russia, whose peasant soldiers in March 1917 turned on the regime that had driven them into slaughter and their families to starvation. Italy withdrew from the war later that year. But by then shiploads of U.S. soldiers were crossing the Atlantic to join the British and French. At first the Americans had declared themselves strictly neutral. But when Russia collapsed they intervened to stop Germany from crushing the French and British and becoming the only major power in Europe.

Of World War I, MacArthur later said, its "ferocity and magnitude of losses were unequalled in the history of humanity" to that time. Over the previous century, while they had fought no major wars, Europeans had nonetheless transformed the nature of combat. Once the concern of a relatively small group of arms makers and career soldiers, by the 20th century, war between major powers meant mobilization of a country's entire economy and able-bodied population. Virtually all of Europe's young men were put into uniform and sent to face the withering firepower and deadly chemistry of the industrialized battlefield with its machine guns, long-range artillery, and poison gas. They died by the millions.

Thanks to artillery, the killing zone extended for miles on both sides of a battle front. Thanks to the machine gun, a few men defending a position could wipe out hundreds, even thousands, of attackers. This one innovation, as MacArthur wrote, drove "great armies into a stalemate of trench and mud." Gas attacks and massive artillery barrages devastated both sides without changing the balance of power.

By 1917 the United States was the most powerful country in the world economically; its industry and agriculture produced more than any other country's. During the war this strong peacetime economy underwent a tremendous mobilization to become the world's most powerful war machine as well. In these years Douglas MacArthur's career took off, and he rose into the upper ranks of a blossoming military establishment.

Thanks to an old friend of General Arthur MacArthur II, Douglas's rapid ascent began just a few months after his father died. General Leonard Wood had served with MacArthur in New Mexico and went on to became governor of Cuba after the

Spanish-American War, during the same period that Arthur MacArthur became governor of the Philippines. Like other top officers, Wood was well aware of how Taft had kept Arthur MacArthur from becoming commander of the army in 1907.

Wood was given this position himself in 1910, when Taft was president. In 1912 he made a decision to help Arthur's grieving family. The oldest son, Arthur III, was then stationed in Washington, D.C., living there with his wife, Mary, and their four children. In December Wood assigned Douglas to be his own aide, making it possible for the brothers and their mother to be reunited in the nation's capital.

Wood moved Douglas between a number of different assignments, from managing the War and State Departments' office building to planning training and mobilization of citizen reservists. This last job "attracted me most," MacArthur later wrote, and inspired him to toil "as Wood's assistant in his indefatigable crusade for military preparedness." Deeply impressed by Wood and knowing what his father's comrade had done and could do for him, MacArthur fawned over his boss and worked avidly. Wood was also impressed with his "highly intelligent and very efficient" aide. Late in 1913 he moved MacArthur to a staff position working in war planning and training. And in 1914 Wood turned quickly to his trusted captain when President Woodrow Wilson ordered the army to prepare for fighting in Mexico.

Early in 1914 a chaotic civil war broke out in Mexico between a military regime and a deeply divided revolutionary movement. In April, President Wilson ordered U.S. forces to occupy the port city of Veracruz on the Gulf of Mexico to stop an arms shipment to the Mexican army. He also ordered Wood to step down as chief of the army and take personal command of a "possible expeditionary force" that would prepare to enter Mexico through Veracruz and seize the capital of Mexico City.

Wood immediately sent MacArthur to Veracruz to learn all that an invader would need to know. Arriving a week later, MacArthur sneaked out of the city as a spy, looking for railroad locomotives the army would need to haul men and supplies inland. Armed only with a revolver, MacArthur fought off three attacks by armed bands of Mexicans, killing several men, and located the locomotives. Amazingly, he had bullet holes in his clothes but none in his body.

On his return to Veracruz MacArthur wrote a flattering note to Wood voicing the hope that there would be fighting in Mexico and that it would do the same for Wood's career as a Mexican campaign in the previous century did for General Zachary Taylor. "I miss the inspiration, my dear General, of your own clear-cut, decisive methods. I hope sincerely that affairs will shape themselves so that you will shortly take the field for the campaign which, if death does not call you, can have but one ending—the White House."

But Wilson held off the invasion and the situation in Mexico calmed down. MacArthur returned to Washington in August, as Europe went to war. He remained there the next three years while the army, first quietly and then with increasing urgency, prepared to intervene in Europe.

MacArthur worked on everything from national defense legislation to the replacing of horses and wagons with trucks. He was promoted to major in 1915 and impressed Newton D. Baker, a reform-minded former mayor of Cleveland whom Wilson appointed secretary of war in 1916. That year Baker chose MacArthur to head a new information bureau that Baker set up to concentrate on public relations. Working through the news media, MacArthur remembered, "I was expected to explain our national military policy to the country and to shatter the prevailing delusion of a world living in security." He made himself available to reporters at all hours of the day and, as a group of them wrote to Baker, "helped, through us, to shape the public mind" in the months leading up to war. Throughout the rest of his career MacArthur would show a keen regard for the mass media as a means to communicate with millions of people.

As he rose through the ranks of the army, Douglas and his mother lived well in Washington. They saw a lot of Arthur III and his family and had many other friends and diversions in the capital city. Thanks in part to an inheritance from her family, Pinky was fairly well off. She and her younger son shared a comfortable home and a limousine.

As the war in Europe loomed in 1917 there was disagreement within the U.S. army over how to fight it. The majority of the headquarters staff considered the National Guard inferior and wanted it excluded from an American expeditionary force to Europe. The guard was based on part-time soldiers who spent most of their time as ordinary civilians, except for brief periods of training. Critics claimed these men could not operate as a professional force. But, MacArthur wrote, he "steadfastly shared [his] father's belief in the citizen-soldier."

MacArthur argued that without the National Guard the country could not bring enough strength to bear in time to stop Germany and win the war. There was considerable disagreement. But Baker sided with MacArthur and took him to the White House, where they convinced President Wilson that the United States could rely on the National Guard. MacArthur later suggested that Baker form a special division of guard "units from the different states so that a division would stretch over the whole country like a rainbow." Baker not only agreed, he promoted MacArthur to major and assigned him to be chief of staff for the new division's commander. The 26,000-man Rainbow Division sailed for France in October 1917.

The Rainbow was one of the few American divisions on hand to face an all-out German offensive beginning in March 1918. Knowing that many more Americans were on the way, Germany tried desperately to win before they arrived. The division fought at numerous sections of the front, from the Marne River just east of Paris to the Meurthe River north of the Swiss border.

MacArthur carefully organized his work at the division headquarters so that he was not tied down there and could spend much of his time on the front lines. In May Francis Duffy, a chaplain with the division, wrote in his diary that MacArthur had become controversial: "Our chief of staff chafes at his own task of directing instead of fighting, and he has pushed himself into raids and forays in which, some older heads think, he had no business to be. His admirers say that his personal boldness has a very valuable result in helping to give confidence to the men." But MacArthur and those who agreed with him "are wild Celts," Duffy concluded, "whose opinion no sane man like myself would uphold."

While her son fought in France, in Washington Pinky MacArthur used her acquaintance with the American commander in France, General John J. Pershing, in an effort to have Douglas promoted. When Pinky and Arthur MacArthur had journeyed to Asia in 1905 they had shared the monthlong voyage across the Pacific with Pershing and his new bride. In 1917 Pinky wrote Pershing, as she put it " . . . a little heart-to-

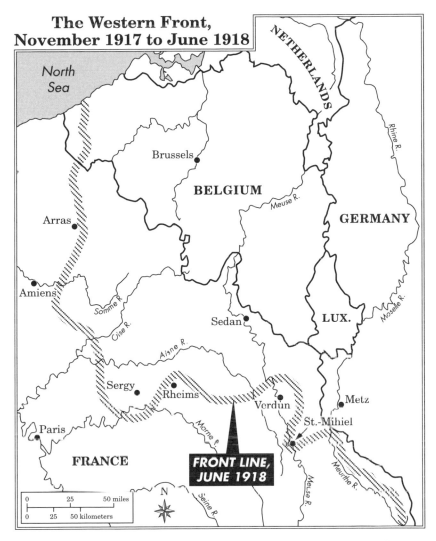

The western front of World War I in France, showing the limits of the German offensive against Paris and the areas where Douglas MacArthur and the Rainbow Division fought

heart letter . . . I know the secretary of War and his family quite intimately, and the Secretary is very deeply attached to Colonel MacArthur . . . My hope and ambition in life is to live long enough to see this son made a General Officer, and I feel I am placing my entire life, as it were, in your hands . . ." Whether because of Pinky's plea or not, Pershing approved Douglas's promotion to brigadier general in June 1918.

The next month Douglas's frontline style brought him face-to-face with the full horror of industrialized warfare. Outside the town of Chalons, roughly 100 miles northeast of Paris, the Rainbow Division helped to break a final German assault that became a slaughter. MacArthur joined fellow officers in celebrating the victory, but without enthusiasm. "It may have been the vision of those writhing bodies hanging from the barbed wire or the stench of dead flesh . . . Somehow, I had forgotten how to play."

This vision of war grew even worse when the Rainbow Division attacked toward the Marne and Ourcq Rivers, where their recent offensives had brought the Germans dangerously close to Paris. By the time the Rainbow arrived at this section of the front in late July to take the village of Sergy on the Ourcq, the Germans had begun a deadly retreat. MacArthur remembered:

> They massed machine guns and mortars behind rugged stone walls and in scattered farm buildings. Our artillery was not in sufficient strength to silence this death blaze of Germany. Death beckoned the bravest and the strongest in the deceptive fields of that bright green countryside . . . Crawling forward in twos and threes against each stubborn nest of enemy guns, we closed in with the bayonet and the hand grenade . . . A point would be taken, and then would come sudden fire from some unsuspected direction and the deadly counterattack. Positions changed hands time and again. There was neither rest nor mercy.

In the midst of this fighting MacArthur was freed from his headquarters responsibilities as chief of staff and was put in command of one of the Rainbow Division's two infantry brigades, the 84th. Its authorized strength of 8,500 had dwindled to about 5,000 men.

The Germans made a bitter stand at Meurcy Farm, near Sergy, and then broke with the Americans hard on their heels. In early August, when MacArthur's brigade pulled out after nine days of furious combat, it had melted away to 2,300 able-bodied men. "Back came our decimated battalions along the way they had already traveled," Chaplain Duffy wrote. "They marched in wearied silence until they came to the slopes around Meurcy Farm. Then from end to end of the line came the sound of dry, suppressed sobs" as the men passed a field littered with the bodies of their comrades.

The division replenished its ranks with fresh men and soon joined in other battles as bloody as the one around Sergy. The struggle went on through October, as American troops poured to the front and the German armies reeled back. The fighting ended November 6, 1918 with an Germany's surrender.

MacArthur was put in command of the entire Rainbow Division. He led his men from what he called "the blood-soaked fields of France" to join in the occupation of Germany. Of 26,000 men in the Rainbow, only two out of five returned home physically unscathed; nearly one in five died.

MacArthur's memories of this conflict would never fade, and his efforts to interpret and explain the sacrifice he witnessed would dominate his thought on war from then on. Seventeen years later, in a speech to the Rainbow's veterans, he described his soldiers facing death, in words tinged with pride and anguish.

> In memory's eye I see them now—forming grimly for the attack, blue-lipped, covered with sludge and mud, chilled by the wind and rain of the fox hole, driving home to their objective, and to the judgment seat of God . . . They died unquestioning, uncomplaining, with faith in their hearts and on their lips the hope that we would go on to victory.
>
> Never again for them staggering columns, bending under soggy packs, on many a weary march from dripping dusk to drizzling dawn. Never again will they slug ankle deep through the mud of shellshocked roads. Never again will they stop cursing their luck long enough to whistle through chapped lips a few bars . . . Never again ghastly trenches with their maze of tunnels, drifts, pits, dugouts—never again gentlemen unafraid.

While in occupied Germany MacArthur expressed hope to the famous writer William Allen White that the Great War would make possible an enduring peace. "I had never before met so vivid, so captivating, so magnetic a man," White wrote.

> He stood six feet, had a clean-shaven face, a clean-cut mouth, nose and chin, lots of brown hair, good eyes . . . His staff adored him, his men worshipped him . . . He felt the

> common people of Germany had war crammed so far down
> into their bellies that it had gone into their legs, and they
> were done with it and all who advocated it. He said the
> German women were all voters and were studying poli-
> tics . . .

Enfranchised women, MacArthur hoped, would prove to be a strong antiwar force in Germany.

Woodrow Wilson had named the conflict the war to end all wars. Like MacArthur, he linked democratic ideals to hopes of peace. The president's advocacy of human rights inspired millions around the world. But when world leaders gathered to formally end the war they imposed humiliating and economically crushing terms on the defeated Germans. MacArthur's optimism changed to dismay. "We are wondering here what is to happen with reference to the peace terms," he wrote a friend in May 1919 after returning to Washington. "They look drastic and seem to me more like a treaty of perpetual war . . ."

6

EMPTY VICTORIES
1919–1932

The tall, young brigadier general danced gracefully in the ballroom at one of New York City's finest hotels, the Waldorf-Astoria. He wore full dress uniform and glossy black boots with shining spurs. He was a hero, just returned that spring of 1919 from helping to win the Great War, and the medals on his chest left no doubt of his courage. He was an honored guest, but the hotel had its rules and the maitre d' had to enforce them. So he interrupted the officer and his dance partner. The Waldorf did not allow the wearing of spurs on its polished dance floor, he explained politely.

The brigadier general looked at the headwaiter in amazement. "Do you know who I am?" he asked. Of course, the apologetic maitre d' replied, whereupon Douglas MacArthur strode with his partner from the Waldorf—never, he said, to return.

He did not tolerate insults—whether real or imagined—very well. But for a decade or more after the Great War MacArthur endured what he saw as profoundly offensive and blind indifference toward the threat of war. In the 1920s and early 1930s it seemed to him that the country indeed did not recognize its soldiers as guardians of freedom and tried to simply wish away the very existence of war.

MacArthur climbed through the upper ranks of an increasingly feeble army. He watched as tanks, airplanes, and more

Major General Douglas MacArthur in 1930, when he was army chief of staff
(MacArthur Memorial Archives)

powerful artillery continued to increase the destructiveness and range of weapons and drove the costs of preparedness up while military spending fell. In 1930 he reached the top of his profession to win the job that was denied to his father, only to take command of the army as its size and condition reached new lows.

As World War I ended, it did not look at first as if the army would go into decline. MacArthur returned to a hero's welcome at the War Department in Washington. The Rainbow Division had vindicated the army's faith in the National Guard. Newton Baker, who was still secretary of war, admired MacArthur more than ever and appointed him the superintendent of West Point, one of the most prestigious jobs a young general could hope for. In June 1919 MacArthur moved into the superintendent's house on the academy grounds; and, just as she had accompanied her son when he enrolled as a cadet 20 years before, Pinky came, too.

There was little so sacred to Douglas as the corps of cadets, the "long gray line" of West Point officers. But the academy's course of study had been cut and condensed during the war in a crash effort to speed cadets to the army. Worse yet, the academy's program was falling further and further behind the momentous changes taking place in warfare. Baker wanted the academy brought up to date.

It was clear to the new superintendent that a relatively small professional force was no longer enough to win a major war; it took a huge military organization that drew on the entire economy and population of a country for arms production, supply, and combat. Because a modern army was too big and costly to maintain continuously, MacArthur reasoned, it must have the ability to pull itself together quickly in time of emergency, relying largely on masses of citizens. The seed from which this army would spring would be a group of the very best, most versatile, and well-prepared officers, able to mobilize, train, inspire, and lead the millions of citizen soldiers. These men, MacArthur wrote in his first year at the academy, must have "an intimate understanding of the mechanics of human feelings, and a comprehensive grasp of world and national affairs." Their education should "develop initiative and force of character rather than automatic performance of stereotyped functions . . ."

After he took over as superintendent MacArthur reduced the traditional isolation of cadets within the academy grounds. He tried to promote the teaching of history, writing, and foreign languages and to move from an emphasis on memorization and recitation to analysis and discussion. But the superintendent did not have the sort of authority over his faculty that a general has over his officers. Though able to irritate and shake the faculty up somewhat, he could not transfer or dismiss its members at will. Secure in their positions, with their department heads controlling decisions on courses and teaching methods, the academy faculty stonewalled or ignored most of the superintendent's ideas.

MacArthur had more power outside the classroom. To teach teamwork and fortitude, he made athletics mandatory for every cadet. MacArthur turned to a popular, steel-eyed teacher of Spanish to make athletics work. Matthew B. Ridgway was not much older than the cadets were, having graduated from the academy in 1917. He was a natural leader with a zeal for winning. "He brought me in to take charge of the Athletic Department," Ridgway later said. "He told me right to my face to report only to him."

MacArthur was able to get money from Congress to restore the cuts made during the war. But not only did he face resistance within the academy on how to prepare cadets, he found support for the very idea of war readiness was fading quickly in the country and in Congress. A majority in Congress had little interest in either diplomatic engagement with the world or in military preparedness. The Senate rejected U.S. membership in the League of Nations (an international organization set up with the idea of preventing war), dashing Woodrow Wilson's dream of the United States leading the world into an era of freedom and peace. MacArthur got nowhere with pleas for expansion of the academy's enrollment.

Leaders came to power who did not care to hear warnings from the academy superintendent that failure to prepare the next generation of military leaders might well "be paid for in the bitterness of American blood . . ." Warren Harding, the advocate of "normalcy," entered the White House in March 1921. By September the army had decided to appoint a less troublesome general to run West Point.

Years later MacArthur commented on these experiences when he wrote to a friend: "The more you become acquainted with the bureaucracy of our governmental departments the more pessimistic you will become. 'Red tape,' 'Bureaucracy,' 'Routine,' 'Laissez faire'—whatever you wish to call it—its deadening effect is felt by everyone who comes within the scope of its influence."

In late 1921, not long after MacArthur learned he would be leaving the academy, Louise Cromwell Brooks went on vacation. She left her magnificent estate in the Baltimore area, which she called Rainbow Hill, and headed for a luxury resort in the beautiful valley of the Hudson River, near West Point. There the 42-year-old divorcée met the 41-year-old general, and they fell for one another immediately.

Louise was heiress to a multimillion-dollar fortune—based partly on the business empire of the J.P. Morgan Company. She enjoyed the companionship of many powerful people in the business world and in the army. When the Americans went to war in France, she and her first husband entertained General John Pershing and other top commanders in Paris. Louise and her husband divorced after the war but she continued to welcome Pershing and other generals in the Washington area to receptions and parties at Rainbow Hill.

Having known each other but a few months, Louise Brooks and Douglas MacArthur married in February 1922. That fall they left for the Philippines.

Over the next eight years MacArthur was stationed in the Philippines twice, for two years in the early 1920s and two years at the end of the decade. He commanded forces in the Manila area through 1924. Upon his promotion to major general in early 1925 he and Louise went back to the United States, where he spent most of the next four years as commander of troops in Washington, D.C. and the surrounding area. In 1927 Louise left him with the servants at Rainbow Hill and moved to New York City. In the fall of 1928 he sailed for the islands once again, this time to be U.S. commander in the Philippines. Louise did not go with him and divorced him the next year.

What information there is about the marriage suggests that the infatuation Douglas and Louise had for one another faded after a few years, and they eventually found that they had little in common. To a woman enamored of the military, MacArthur was certainly impressive, and he was comfortable among the wealthy and powerful. He also grew very fond of Louise's two children. But he had little interest in the business world of her family and friends, and she had little interest in his world in the Philippines.

The failure of the marriage followed other personal sorrows for MacArthur. Pinky developed heart trouble in 1923. She improved after Douglas rushed home from the islands briefly to see her, but she remained frail. In December, after Douglas returned to Manila, word came that Arthur MacArthur III had suddenly developed appendicitis and died while on duty in Washington. The world had begun "to seem a very lonesome place," MacArthur wrote to a friend. His only brother had followed their father, leaving Douglas alone with their invalid mother. Pinky stayed in Washington with Arthur's widow, Mary, and Mary's children.

Along with his loneliness, MacArthur was frustrated in his work by the continuing stagnation and decline of the army. During his time in the Philippines the general worked with a shrinking force occupying a deeply divided country. American rule brought some forms of democracy to the islands, including an elected legislature. But it only embittered conflict between rich landowners and poor peasants, which was the heritage of Spanish rule. The peasants rented the land they tilled. In bad years they had no choice but to borrow from their landlords in order to get by. Debt accumulated and passed from generation to generation, binding the peasants ever more securely to their poverty and their landlords.

The gulf between landowners and landless deepened after the United States conquered the Philippines, according to a report by the American State Department in 1950. The United States stopped taxing goods from the islands as it did imports from foreign countries. Filipino landowners began to concentrate on producing cash crops for the American market and on involvement in the colonial government. They "acquired a near monopoly of political power," according to the report. "Tenants, as a rule, did not share in the political emancipation of the country. They did not enjoy freedom of speech and assemblage, could not join organizations of their own choosing and were compelled to vote according to the political affiliation of the landowner."

To keep the peasants in line, landlords relied on armed gangs and also on the Philippine Constabulary, the Filipino police force Taft had organized under the colonial government. Arthur MacArthur II had opposed having the U.S. Army and the constabulary share the same territory as two independent military forces. He had favored bringing Filipinos into the army. This later happened on a small scale. About 3,500 of these native troops, known as Philippine Scouts, came under the command of Douglas MacArthur in 1923. They were members of the U.S. Philippine Division, with a total of 7,000 soldiers. In 1924 MacArthur became commander of the division, which accounted for about half of all U.S. troops in the islands. Scouts sometimes helped quell violence in the countryside, but they were not identified as enemies of the peasants. Besides training to be expert marksmen, gunners, and military engineers, they worked at such peaceful pursuits as vaccinating livestock against disease.

Like his father, Douglas MacArthur did not comment on or try to change the deep divisions within Filipino society. But he did express sympathy with Filipino aspirations for independence and let his Scouts know that he favored equal treatment for them within the U.S. Army. Scouts received much lower pay and benefits than Americans in the same army and endured numerous other forms of discrimination. They resented it so much that more than 200 of them went on strike in 1923 and were court-martialed and imprisoned for mutiny. This caused quite a stir among some Americans, who began to fear that a rebellion was coming.

Most Westerners in the islands considered natives worthy of no more than a token role in the government and did not associate as equals even with the wealthiest Filipinos. The goal of independence, the general wrote, "was being challenged by foreign forces within the country, as indeed was the goal of equal social status. Attitudes die hard and the old idea of colonial exploitation still had its vigorous supporters. As a result of my friendly relations with Filipinos, there began to appear a feeling of resentment, even antagonism, against me . . ."

MacArthur maintained close ties to Manuel Quezon, president of the Filipino Senate and the most powerful figure in the islands' politics, who had met MacArthur back in 1904. Wealthy and educated, Quezon was a colorful, charming, and shrewd leader. Millions believed in him as a symbol of Filipino pride and a fiery advocate of independence, but in practice he was cautious in his pursuit of this goal. Living in a U.S. possession gave Filipino landowners access to the lucrative American market. And also, Quezon believed, this status gave the Philippines insurance against the growing strength of another power in the Pacific: Japan.

Japan's imperialists, somewhat like their American counterparts, argued that their country needed an Asian empire for security and prosperity. After defeating Russia in 1904, the Japanese dominated Korea. In 1910 the Japanese formally annexed the country. Then, after the Great War broke out in Europe in 1914, Japan seized all of Germany's possessions in the Pacific region including a port in China and a number of islands in the Pacific.

Within the Japanese empire the government—and particularly the army—conceded nothing to the rights, culture, or lives of the people who came within their power. Their rule over Korea demonstrated brute exploitation of a conquered people. The totalitarianism that prevailed in the empire also grew within Japan. In 1925 the government adopted its first "Peace Preservation Law," which began to limit freedom of speech, political action, and even thought.

Though Quezon championed Philippine independence in public to win elections, he actually pursued a more gradual approach, in which Filipinos moved toward racial equality and political power *within* the colonial government, and the islands could look forward to eventual independence under safer conditions. The American governor of the Philippines in the early 1920s was MacArthur's old friend and benefactor, Leonard Wood. He rebuffed Quezon's initiatives; and the two men became bitter enemies.

MacArthur showed Filipinos a somewhat kinder American face, in part because they remembered his father's treatment of Emilio Aguinaldo and support of self-government. The Scouts' loyalty to MacArthur allowed the general to keep these troops in line after the mutiny and to reassure Wood. When

Wood died and was replaced by a more diplomatic governor, relations with Quezon and the Filipinos improved.

In the United States, meanwhile, leaders did not share Quezon's concerns about Japan. A Democrat named Franklin D. Roosevelt, who had run unsuccessfully for the vice presidency, wrote in the early 1920s that war fears were based on an "old outlook . . . The whole trend of the times is against wars for colonial expansion. The thought of the world leans the other way." As Japan grew to become the strongest Pacific power, U.S. strength in the islands during the late 1920s went down to about 12,000 troops and a few gunboats and destroyers. The nearest source of potential reinforcement, Hawaii, was thousands of miles away.

Not only did the United States have little interest in defending the Philippines, its most distant possession, it did little even to protect Washington. Most of the time that MacArthur was stationed in the country, from 1925 through late 1928, he commanded the military district around the capital and Baltimore. He found a neglected network of shore and river defenses and soldiers poorly housed and undersupplied with obsolete and worn equipment. The country was embracing a variety of ideas—from pacifism to isolationism—that produced a climate of opinion against preparedness. In Washington as at West Point, MacArthur turned to athletics, organizing competitions to keep up the morale of his soldiers.

MacArthur's enthusiasm for sports helped to gain him appointment in 1927 as head of the U.S. Olympic Committee. He led American athletes to the games at Amsterdam in 1928. He told them at one point: "We did not come here to lose gracefully, we came to win." They dominated the competition.

The next year MacArthur showed interest in pursuing high office outside of the army. Soon after taking command of U.S. forces in the Philippines, late in 1928, the general tried to land the post of governor. Henry L. Stimson, Wood's successor in that position, left for Washington to become secretary of state in the administration of the new American president, Herbert Hoover. MacArthur asked Quezon for support in getting the job and even suggested what Quezon should write in a recommendation. The Filipino people had "almost unanimous agreement on General MacArthur," MacArthur wrote. "I know of no man who so thoroughly commands the confidence both of the

American people and the Filipinos. His appointment would be a master stroke . . ."

"According to close friends," a reporter for the *New York Times* wrote in April of 1929, "General MacArthur has his eyes on the White House for eight or twelve years hence, via a successful administration as [Philippines] Governor General for four years and then four years in a Cabinet post, either as Secretary of State or Secretary of War."

President Hoover showed no interest in naming MacArthur governor of the Philippines, but in 1930 Hoover chose him to be commanding general of the army. The president made his decision, he said, after he "searched the army for younger blood."

By this time it had become clear that the United States and the world were in the grip of an unprecedented economic collapse, the Great Depression. MacArthur knew that the already minimal army budget would be slashed in the crisis. "I did not want to return to Washington," he wrote " . . . I knew the dreadful ordeal that faced the new chief of staff, and shrank from it . . . But my mother . . . sensed what was in my mind and cabled me to accept. She said my father would be ashamed if I showed timidity. That settled it."

Arriving in Washington late in 1930, MacArthur took the oath to become army chief of staff and settled into a home with Pinky. He wrote declarations of love and devotion to Isabel Cooper, a young Filipino dancer and singer he had become involved with in Manila. She agreed to follow him to Washington, where the relationship disintegrated. They had enjoyed an active and public social life in the islands, but in Washington MacArthur isolated his lover in an apartment to hide the affair from the public and above all from his mother. Isabel rebelled, and they separated. Eventually she took a bribe for her silence and left Washington. MacArthur narrowly missed a public embarrassment that would have frozen his army career. Thirty years later Isabel died, alone, in California.

MacArthur took command of the army as the depression rapidly worsened to become an economic disaster. Joblessness, poverty, and hunger mushroomed. The country turned ever more deeply into isolationism, as Europe and Asia turned toward war. Armies and navies around the world fielded new guns, planes, ships, and submarines. Improved tanks and other armored machines were destroying the defensive power of the machine gun. "It was plain to see that modern war would be a war of massive striking power, a war of lightning movement, a war of many machines," MacArthur later wrote.

How a small army with a diminishing budget should spend its money in the face of these developments became a bitterly contested issue. The new machinery of war was very expensive to develop and manufacture. Airplanes in particular required such precision in the making of their high-speed motors that they spawned a revolution in metalworking industries. MacArthur had to deal with factions in the army and in Congress that pressed for development of armored units, fighter planes, bombers, antiaircraft defense, and for cuts in the numbers of soldiers.

When MacArthur became commander, the army had declined to 135,000 men, less than half the force that the government had established at the end of World War I. With the technology of war changing so rapidly, MacArthur insisted, the army could not afford expensive weapons that would soon become obsolete. It must instead preserve a core of trained officers and men, continue research and development, and be ready to begin mass production of weapons and machines quickly if war threatened. The general was especially tenacious in fending off attempts to reduce the army's 12,000-man officer corps. Congress devoted more money to air power than MacArthur sought, but by and large he prevailed.

Then, in 1931, war became a reality in Asia. Japan's army invaded north from Korea, into the huge Chinese province of Manchuria. The first of the violence known today as World War II had begun. MacArthur urged President Hoover to lead an international campaign against Japan's trade. But this, the president concluded, might provoke war. The United States and the rest of the world continued to sell the Japanese a variety of goods, including essential war materials such as oil and metals. Within Japan the army and navy undermined and eventually destroyed civilian rule through intrigue, mutiny, assassination, and rebellion.

Hoover was increasingly preoccupied with the desperate domestic situation. As the president pressed for more cutbacks, MacArthur grasped for another path toward security: disarmament. In the spring of 1932 the general met with members of a U.S. delegation as they prepared for negotiations in Europe. MacArthur was at that time chairman of the Army-Navy board, making him the top uniformed spokesman of the military establishment. He urged the delegation to try to make offensive warfare virtually impossible against all but the lightest of defenses, according to notes by one of the diplomats present. Because of the huge industrial base required to make modern weapons and other military equipment, he said,

> the whole tendency of war . . . was to regard it as a struggle between whole nations rather than between professional organizations. Effectively to arm all nations or to provide the Army and Navy with weapons that could subdue an entire nation was beyond the economic scope of any power and was more than any other factor driving the world into bankruptcy . . . Our ultimate aim should be to obtain an agreement on the part of all nations that they would give no government support in any form to aviation. In other words, to give up military and naval aviation in their entirety . . . He [MacArthur] admitted that this was too radical a solution but felt it should be the ultimate goal.

MacArthur also called for a total ban on mobile artillery. The combined effect of all of his proposals was to virtually eliminate offensive power in war and thereby to limit or even eliminate war as a means of conquest. An attacking army would have no airplanes or heavy guns with which to destroy the fixed artillery and fortifications of the army defending its own borders.

Some weeks later Jay Pierrepont Moffat, the same diplomat who had jotted down notes of MacArthur's arguments, mentioned the general's concept to Secretary of State Henry L. Stimson. The secretary, Moffat wrote, was astonished.

> Muttering to himself that it was impossible that we quoted him accurately, he seized the telephone receiver and asked the Chief of Staff if he could come around for a few moments . . . We were treated to the unusual spectacle of the head of the War Department [MacArthur] arguing for a decrease in a military arm while the head of the so-called peace department was attempting to prove him wrong . . . When he left the Secretary blew up, . . . said that he was predominantly concerned with his budget.

Hoover was desperate enough to try the idea, but Mac-Arthur's victory within the administration in this dispute proved empty. The negotiations fizzled, leaving MacArthur frustrated, struggling to maintain a fragment of military potential.

Some of the MacArthur's work during the 1920s was to prove decisive. His ideas about training officers took hold gradually at West Point. The core group of officers that he fought to preserve through the Great Depression later built an army that helped to make the United States the dominant power in a very different world after World War II.

But in 1932 these successes were not apparent. Japan was bringing war to Asia, the rise of fascism in Germany was beginning to threaten peace in Europe, the United States was weak, and the Great Depression had plunged its people into misery and turmoil.

SMILES OF YESTERDAY
1932–1942

Major Dwight D. Eisenhower insisted that it would be "highly inappropriate" for the country's top general to join troops who were going to suppress a riot. But the general, who had gotten into the habit of sometimes speaking of himself in the third person, declared: "MacArthur will take the field." He changed from his impeccable white suit into full uniform and said he must be on hand to deal with the "incipient revolution in the air," according to the major.

By that day, July 28, 1932, idleness, poverty, and hunger stalked millions. Many people worried about where the Great Depression might take a grim and shaken country. But, besides MacArthur, hardly anyone believed a few thousand poor veterans would or could overthrow the government. After all, they had come to Washington to ask for that government's money.

They were the Bonus Army, tens of thousands of veterans from the Great War. Jobless and desperate, they marched on Washington from around the country that spring, many with their families, calling for early payment of a bonus Congress had promised they would receive in their old age. These men had survived the horrors of war in their youth only to fall victim to poverty and despair in the depression. A writer, John Dos Passos, described their "sunken eyes, hollow cheeks off breadlines, pale-looking knotted hands of men who've worked hard with them, and then for a long time have not worked."

They set up makeshift camps on the outskirts of Washington, the largest of them at Anacostia Flats on the Potomac River. Congress had come up with some of the bonus money. But, though the marchers lobbied and demonstrated, they could not obtain the rest. Some gave up and went home. But tension and frustration mounted in the summer heat and a few bands of self-styled revolutionaries tried to intervene in the demonstrations. In a confrontation with some of the remaining bonus marchers the morning of July 28 near Capitol Hill, police panicked and killed two men. Within hours a nervous President Herbert Hoover ordered the army to drive the marchers from the city.

For the past three years MacArthur had been watching over a declining army while, as he saw it, threats arose on every side: war, revolution, tyranny, and chaos overseas; isolationists, bureaucrats, pacifists, labor agitators, and leftists at home. He had spoken out repeatedly, denouncing pacifists in

The ruins of a camp set up by impoverished veterans of World War I on the outskirts of Washington, D.C., burn on July 29, 1932, after troops evicted the veterans on orders from Chief of Staff Douglas MacArthur. (MacArthur Memorial Archives)

particular as the bedfellows of communists and traitors. Now he concluded that the veterans demonstrating in Washington were not veterans at all but, despite reports of his own spies to the contrary, a mob bent on violent revolution.

On MacArthur's orders 800 troops mobilized near the White House, and he went to the scene himself with his protesting aide Dwight Eisenhower in tow. Armed with rifles, bayonets, sabers, and tear gas, the men moved down Pennsylvania Avenue in the direction of the Capitol and the two vacant buildings that the veterans had occupied. Mounted horsemen clattered down the streets of Washington. Machine guns and even a few small tanks stood ready.

That evening, after his soldiers had teargassed a baby to death and driven the marchers to their camp at Anacostia Flats, MacArthur refused to receive instructions the president had sent by way of the War Department. Hoover wanted the army to stop. But the man who claimed to be protecting the president's authority "said he was too busy and did not want either himself or his staff bothered by people coming down and pretending to bring orders," Eisenhower wrote. The soldiers stopped for supper and then advanced on Anacostia Flats. They chased several thousand American veterans and their families into the night and set fire to the camp. Hoover quickly endorsed the actions of his high-handed general.

The next morning, at the New York state capital in Albany, Governor Franklin D. Roosevelt looked over the accounts and photos of the confrontation in his morning newspaper. Because of this, the Democratic presidential nominee told an aide, his last doubts about winning the election that fall had vanished. Hoover, already on the ropes politically because of the country's desperate economic situation, had just finished himself off by enraging veterans nationwide over the treatment of their impoverished comrades.

The president who had put MacArthur at the head of the army—and who might have advanced him further still—lost the election decisively that November. But the general who thought he smelled revolution in the air of Washington also perceived truly menacing trends on both the eastern and western horizons of the United States—in Europe and in Asia—trends that most of the country's leaders could not or would not see. MacArthur's concern about maintaining the foundation of an army in the face of these threats turned to desperation soon after Roosevelt's inauguration in March 1933. And in his desperation the discredited villain of the Bonus March incident managed to exert some influence within the new administration.

Roosevelt, as he rushed proposals to Congress for emergency spending on jobs and other economic programs, embraced MacArthur's disarmament plan. "If all nations will agree wholly to eliminate from possession and use the weapons which make possible a successful attack, defenses will automatically become impregnable, and the frontiers and independence of every nation will become secure," the president declared in a ringing message to world leaders on May 16.

To many leaders this message brought hope to a gloomy situation. The democratic civilian governments of two major powers had become hollow fronts for aggressive dictatorships. In January 1933 Adolf Hitler took power in Germany. In February, when the League of Nations formally ruled that Japan committed aggression in Manchuria, the Japanese walked out of the league as their army pressed on into northern China. Hitler noticed that neither the United States nor any member of the league sought to punish Japan in any way for its aggression. American isolationists insisted on a policy of strict "neutrality."

Roosevelt's message of security through offensive disarmament brought universal praise. Even Hitler called the message a "ray of comfort." Germany, he said, "does not think of attacking but only of acquiring security." The president told a friend, "I think I have averted a war."

But Roosevelt did not intend to wait for negotiations before cutting the military, as MacArthur had planned. The administration's Bureau of the Budget announced plans to reduce the army's funding by one-third. The president thought of this as a goodwill gesture to the world that would also help pay for his urgently needed economic programs.

Roosevelt's own secretary of war, former Utah governor George Dern, was shocked. He summoned MacArthur, and they went to the White House to see the president. MacArthur had toured Europe in 1931 and 1932, and he was sure that Hitler intended to rearm Germany and try to dominate Europe.

He was equally worried about Japanese aggression in Asia and, potentially, in the Pacific.

MacArthur and Roosevelt first met in Washington before World War I, when the future president worked for the navy. They met again that spring of 1933 in the Oval Office as two desperate men—the harried president reaching for every possible resource to get the country moving again and the chief of staff trying to save an army he believed must protect the country from an even greater danger than the depression.

Roosevelt spoke acidly to Dern about the folly and the cost of maintaining a peacetime army while the country fell apart from within. "Under his lashing tongue," MacArthur recalled, "the secretary grew white and silent. I felt it my duty to take up the cudgels. The country's safety was at stake, and I said so bluntly. The president turned the full vials of his sarcasm on me."

Under Roosevelt's goading, MacArthur accused the president of setting the stage for calamity. "When we lose the next war," he told the commander in chief, "and an American boy, lying in the mud with an enemy bayonet through his belly and an enemy foot on his dying throat, spits out his last curse, I want the name not to be MacArthur but Roosevelt."

"You must not talk that way to the president!" a livid Roosevelt roared. MacArthur stammered an apology. "I felt my army career was at an end," he wrote. "I told him he had my resignation as chief of staff." With his stomach heaving from tension, the general turned to leave.

Both men knew by this time that the army was putting jobless men to work more quickly than any civilian branch of the government could. The army under MacArthur was mobilizing 250,000 into the new Civilian Conservation Corps (CCC), outfitting them and distributing them to hundreds of work camps throughout the country. Whether for this or for some other reason, Roosevelt calmed himself quickly. "As I reached the door," MacArthur recalled, "his voice came with that cool detachment which so reflected his extraordinary self-control. 'Don't be foolish, Douglas; you and the Budget [Bureau] must get together on this.'"

MacArthur and Dern were able to hold the army's budget cut to around 10 percent and to avoid further cuts the next year. The president and the general developed a strained

relationship of conflict and collaboration that—far from con-
signing MacArthur to retirement—vaulted him into the leadership role in which he helped shape the world as it is today.

The general worked relentlessly to preserve and prepare the
army. MacArthur's conservatism, army record, and command
of information and language made him persuasive. He lobbied
members of Congress at hearings, in private conversations,
and in memos. He was a counterweight to isolationist leaders,
who continued to gain power in Congress and sought to para-
lyze the president. The president in turn watched disarmament negotiations collapse and became gradually more
concerned about Germany and Japan. Late in 1934, as Mac-
Arthur ended the customary four years of service as chief of
staff, Roosevelt delayed replacing him.

With Germany rearming in open defiance of the Versailles
Peace Treaty of 1919, early in 1935 Roosevelt endorsed Mac-
Arthur's call to increase the size of the army by 30 percent,
from 131,000 to 172,000 men. Congress approved the measure
after a hard-fought struggle. The army was still relatively
small, but it was growing rather than shrinking. Later in 1935
Roosevelt and MacArthur agreed that the general should return to the Philippines to help this vulnerable U.S. territory
face the growing menace of Japan.

Manuel Quezon asked for help on a visit to Washington that
year. In the early 1930s the Filipino leader concluded that it
was no longer possible to contain his people's desire for independence or the desire of American isolationists to be rid of
responsibility for defense of the islands. In 1934 Congress
declared that the Philippines would become independent in
1946. The first step would be the creation of a commonwealth
government in the islands with the election of a legislature and
a president in 1935. They would remain under the authority of
an American governor until independence. Quezon was elected
to be the first president of the new commonwealth while his
rival, Sergio Osmena, won the vice presidency.

How, Quezon asked MacArthur in Washington, could the
islands be secure in the shadow of Japan? The answer, the
general told him, was to make the Philippines a nation of
citizen soldiers trained, organized, and motivated to rally to
their country's defense in an emergency. By training some of
the male population every year and steadily building up stock-

piles of weapons and ammunition, he said, the country would gradually become capable of such massive resistance that it would not be worth the cost of conquest.

Quezon adopted this approach and asked the general to return to the Philippines and guide development of the army for the 10 years of commonwealth government. Roosevelt appointed MacArthur as special adviser to the commonwealth and put the U.S. forces in the islands at his disposal for the purpose of building a new national army around the core of the Philippine Scouts. MacArthur ordered his assistant, Eisenhower, to go along as his top aide.

As he prepared to leave the country and give up the army chief of staff position, MacArthur spoke out once more about preparedness. In a speech July 4 to a convention of Rainbow Division veterans in Washington, he tried to address the stubborn resistance in the country to development of military power. He told the veterans that they had endured sacrifice for the sake of freedom.

MacArthur painted wistful images of the Rainbow soldiers' suffering and triumph in the blood-soaked fields of France. "It was 17 years ago," he told his aging troops. "Those days of old have vanished, tone and tint . . . Their memory is a land where flowers of wondrous beauty and varied colors spring, watered by tears and coaxed and caressed into fuller bloom by the smiles of yesterday."

The horror of war, MacArthur said, could not hide the sacred code that the veterans had served—something he would later call the free man's military code. It was a combination of a commitment to honor, duty, and country, a tradition which "has come down to us from even before the age of knighthood and chivalry," and a devotion to democracy. "The soldier, above all other men, is required to perform the highest act of religious teaching—sacrifice," MacArthur said. " . . . [He] is the noblest development of mankind." The general's description of doomed men (quoted in Chapter Five) gently skirted the actual violence of the battlefield while at the same time painting a stark portrait of misery, and of young lives cut short. Human freedom, he said, springs directly from this terrible loss.

"There is little in our institutions worth having or worth perpetuating that has not been achieved for us by armed men. Trade, wealth, literature, and refinement cannot defend a state—pacific habits do not insure peace . . ." Everyone dreams of a peaceful world, he said, and no one more than the soldier. But, "no wonder that Plato, that wisest of all men, once exclaimed, 'Only the dead have seen the end of war!' . . . As yet it is only a dream."

That fall MacArthur began the trip to Manila as a sad and somewhat humiliated man, despite many honors received in his last days in Washington. Roosevelt, who at times had flattered MacArthur and appeared to be considering him for a high-level appointment outside the army, now seemed eager to be rid of him. Much worse, Pinky MacArthur, who insisted on going with her son though she was in her eighties and weak, became gravely ill as the ship steamed west from San Francisco. Douglas spent many hours by her bedside and many more pacing the deck as she slept. It was on this monthlong trip that, at the age of 55, he met the person who gave him a foundation of personal happiness for the rest of his life.

Jean Faircloth, then 37, came from a prominent family in Murfreesboro, Tennessee. Her father had been a Confederate officer whose soldiers had fought a bloody engagement in the Civil War against Arthur MacArthur's 24th Wisconsin Infantry. While traveling to China to visit friends in the British port of Shanghai, she met a polished and dignified general.

Jean was a delicate, energetic, and naturally cheerful person. She was also intelligent and well educated—quite capable of keeping up with MacArthur. He might well have found her appealing at any time in his stressful life. But as the general watched his mother's health fail out on the vast lonely waters of the Pacific, his relationship with Jean blossomed. She cut her stay in China short and followed MacArthur to Manila.

Pinky died there in early December, a few weeks after she and Douglas arrived. The mother who had planted the seeds of his ambition and become the confidante of a son with few close friends was gone. "Her loss has been a great blow and has filled me with sorrow and distress," he wrote a friend. Years later he added, "of the four of us who had started from the plains of New Mexico, three now were gone, leaving me in my loneliness only a memory of the households we had shared."

Eisenhower noted that months passed before MacArthur's spirits began to recover. Jean, in whose company he loved to enjoy movies and shows almost every night in Manila, helped

Douglas MacArthur, with his top aide Dwight Eisenhower (left of MacArthur) and a small staff, landed in Manila in October of 1935 as the shadow of an aggressive Japan grew darker in Asia and in the western Pacific. His job as military adviser to the Filipinos was to set up the defense of the islands as they prepared for independence. "Without the stability of safety," MacArthur said, "the very foundation of civilization — life, liberty, and the pursuit of happiness — become impossible. It is to assure these to the Filipino people that I am here." (MacArthur Memorial Archives)

dissipate the gloom. And the general soon became absorbed in the task of preparing the Filipinos to defend their islands, as war and preparation for war spread around the world.

MacArthur settled into his headquarters in the massive walls of old Manila and in his penthouse apartment overlooking the bay from the top of the Manila Hotel. Here he planned to make each of the major Philippine islands "a citadel of defensive strength." Having stepped down as army chief of the world's greatest industrial power he inherited the problem that Emilio Aguinaldo and Filipino nationalists had faced when U.S. troops landed in their country back in 1898: How could the poor and scattered Filipino people achieve or maintain independence if a powerful industrial nation, in this case Japan, tried to conquer them?

"Big, lithe Douglas MacArthur," a magazine writer who visited him in late 1936 wrote, "strode around his cool, dim office, set into the thick old walls that, built in 1590, defended Spanish Manila for 327 years.

"Around the room were pictures of military men, American and foreign, one of his father . . . here and there a flag hanging limply on its staff, outside trim staff sergeants and khaki-clad Filipinos battering typewriters in the breeze from electric fans."

"We've been telling the world people can govern themselves democratically," MacArthur told the reporter. "Now we've got to help the Filipinos prove we are right. If the Filipino experiment fails, the prestige of the United States goes down to zero in a world that would like to see us flop anyway. If we let it fail we'll be the world's worst skunks." MacArthur laid out his plan in numerous letters, reports and press interviews. Because of its position on the trade routes of Asia and its status as Asia's only democracy, the security of the Philippines was "necessary to international peace" and "essential to the continued growth and spread of democratic practices" in that part of the world. As in the United States, the citizen soldier fighting in defense of home and liberty was "the keystone of the defensive arch."

He planned to build camps throughout the islands where an average of 40,000 men a year would get six months' basic military training near their homes. With occasional refresher training, this army would grow to a size of 4 million men by the planned date for Filipino independence. By then the islands were to have 250 bombers, to strike an invader's fleet at sea, and 50 torpedo boats for sinking enemy ships as they closed in to land.

"The American army in the islands is just window dressing; the Filipino army will *be* something," MacArthur told the magazine writer. "The Japanese have got Manchuokuo [Manchuria] and Korea and they're getting north China dirt cheap, both in money and lives." But, he said, in the Philippines the cost of conquest would be excessive.

The people MacArthur proposed to train for his army were not citizens of a thriving democracy; they were largely illiterate, poor, isolated peasants and plantation workers, totally unfamiliar with army organization and modern weapons. Many of them were undernourished and diseased. MacArthur despised Roosevelt's New Deal policies designed to help the poor in the United States and fervently hoped for the president's defeat in the 1936 election. But the general's military training program in the Philippines ended up putting a lot of time and money into improving the lot of his impoverished recruits. A pro–New Deal friend of Eleanor Roosevelt, lawyer Frederick C. Howe, wrote to her from the islands of how the men received training "in hygiene, in agriculture, in handicraft, in making them ready to take up homesteads and establish them as self-respecting citizens." He added: "The program being developed by General MacArthur may easily be the nearest guarantee of a permanent peace and a well-grounded democracy . . . that might be made by our government."

But MacArthur had too small a staff, too little money, very little U.S. support, too much to teach his uneducated recruits and, in the end, too little time to build a viable defense. The torpedo boat and bomber programs barely got started. The training program was rushed into full operation with an undersized staff, few training camps, and little equipment. "We have no officer corps," a fuming Eisenhower wrote in his diary, "to supervise organization on such a scale, and officers cannot be produced out of thin air. We have no comprehensive supply system, and we've not yet had a chance to develop the overhead [infrastructure] that can absorb, train, segregate, organize, and maintain reserve units." Pointing out these problems to the general, he continued, only provoked "one of his regular shouting tirades."

Some Filipino units were organized, but most of their members rarely or never fired a gun due to lack of weapons and ammunition.

Back in the United States, the State Department complained to the White House that the general's frequent public statements on the need for preparedness were irritating the Japanese. In September 1937 orders came from the army for MacArthur to return to routine duty in the United States. Instead he retired from the army and accepted Quezon's offer for him to stay on as an employee of the commonwealth government, supervising Eisenhower and the other Americans who continued the training program. At MacArthur's suggestion, Quezon gave him the title of field marshal.

But Quezon was starting to lose faith in the plan of his American friend. That year Japan launched a full-scale invasion of China and seized all its major ports except for the British-controlled city of Hong Kong. Refugees from China reached the Philippines with chilling accounts of Japanese power and savagery. Seeing the lack of U.S. commitment to defend the Philippines, Quezon sank into gloom. He gradually distanced himself from MacArthur, cut money for the training, and visited Tokyo repeatedly seeking to placate the Japanese and get assurances that they would not invade his native land.

MacArthur, who had long respected the power of public opinion, became obsessed with projecting a positive image for his defense program. The Filipinos could defend themselves if only they believed that they could, he wrote Quezon. "All other handicaps can be overcome save that of defeatism." He ordered Eisenhower to answer every negative comment about preparedness in Filipino newspapers. He released glowing progress reports and staged exercises for the press with units of neatly uniformed Filipinos. He exuded confidence to reporters, telling them the Japanese would not be so foolhardy as to attack the Philippines. Eisenhower, meanwhile, returned to army headquarters in Washington to work on preparedness, as the world situation grew increasingly ominous.

Today, in hindsight, the final years before World War II appear as a time of eerie twilight, when the world lived in the shadow of something it had never experienced and could not understand. It was not clear how the conflicts and tensions of Europe and Asia would merge into one global crisis leading to an unprecedented global war. Nor did people comprehend how much technology was expanding the killing zone of the battlefield and the extent of its destructiveness.

For MacArthur, the late 1930s were a twilight filled with happiness. He and Jean married in 1937 and the next year they had a son, the fourth Arthur MacArthur. The family lived well in the hotel penthouse with its stunning view of Manila Bay. The 58-year-old father doted on his only child.

As the decade closed, a cataclysm began. Late in 1939, Hitler made a nonaggression pact with Russian dictator Joseph Stalin, and together they seized and partitioned Poland. The next spring, in 1940, Hitler's armored columns blazed across western Europe. Americans, shocked at Hitler's conquest of a continent, watched in dismay as disaster in Europe set the stage for disaster on the other side of the globe.

After Hitler made peace with Stalin, Japan had no interest in picking a fight on its own with the Soviet Union. But Hitler's conquest of France and Holland, and the desperate situation this caused for the British, gave Japan a much freer hand in southern Asia and in the Malay Archipelago. Soon Tokyo's troops occupied the French territory of northern Vietnam in Indochina. This cut off China's access to ports in Vietnam while at the same time pushing Japan's bases closer to the Malay Archipelago.

Japanese imperialists had dreamed of expelling the Western powers from Asia and seizing their colonies to create a self-sufficient empire. The time had come, officials of the military-controlled government urged their emperor, to wrest the Malay Archipelago from the Americans and the stricken Europeans and thereby to secure sources of oil and other vital goods.

MacArthur saw the looming global struggle. As a retired U.S. officer he was no longer under any obligation to refrain from commenting on national policy, as active officers generally had to do. He joined the bipartisan Committee to Defend America by Aiding the Allies (Russia, Britain, France, and dozens of smaller powers) and became one of its most prominent spokesmen in the effort to quell isolationism and have the United States provide weapons and supplies for the defense of England. It was, he said in a widely disseminated cable of September 1940, a "fight for civilization."

Starting in February of 1941 MacArthur began working with the recently appointed army chief of staff, George C. Marshall, on a crash program to protect the Philippines and use the islands as a platform for devastating attacks on Japan if war came. For defense they planned a combination of troops, batteries of heavy shore guns, mines, torpedo boats, and planes. For offense they planned to build up a large fleet of the world's latest and most destructive war machines: long-range bombers.

In June 1941 Hitler abruptly turned his armies east and launched a devastating attack against Russia on an 800-mile front, breaking his pact with Stalin. The largest-scale fighting of World War II began, consuming lives by the millions. The

U.S. Navy began guarding Britain's vital supply line across the northern Atlantic and began losing ships and men to German submarines. With the navy tied down, Marshall put even higher priority on giving MacArthur overwhelming air power. "With Japan's known preparations to move south," the U.S. army commander wrote in mid-July, "the Philippines became of great strategic importance."

In the last week of July Japan's army and navy began to occupy southern Vietnam, including the city of Saigon and a military base and port at Cam Ranh Bay. Japanese forces were already in position to attack the Philippines from Taiwan. Control of southern Vietnam put them in position to attack into the islands of the Malay Barrier. If they could wipe out American strength on Luzon and defeat the British on the Malay Peninsula and at Singapore, the Japanese could then roll on down the two island chains with practically no opposition, all the way to New Guinea and beyond.

The day after the Japanese took Saigon Roosevelt demanded that they withdraw from Vietnam. He cut off the invader's U.S. trade and seized its assets in the United States. He also drafted all Filipino soldiers into the U.S. Army, returned MacArthur to active duty and made him the U.S. commander in the Philippines. While Roosevelt and MacArthur were not personally or politically close, the president thought of the general as an able fighter who had more Asian experience than any other American military leader.

With the United States on a collision course with both Japan and Germany, Roosevelt secretly boarded a battleship in August and met with England's leader, Winston Churchill, off the coast of Newfoundland. They issued a declaration, the Atlantic Charter, that committed the two powers to a vision of human rights, including the right of all people to freedom and self-government. The statement proclaimed that England and the United States would fight for human freedom—not to preserve or restore the empires of the old imperial powers. Churchill also won a promise from Roosevelt that the defeat of Hitler would take priority over victory in the Pacific.

Hope for peace faded through the fall. In September MacArthur began to call up the Filipino reserves that had been through his training program, a total of about 120,000 men scattered throughout the islands. Marshall rushed to send him

Douglas MacArthur (right) with Manuel Quezon, president of the U.S. Commonwealth of the Philippines, in 1941. MacArthur had retired from the U.S. Army and been hired by Quezon to create a Filipino defense force. MacArthur chose the title field marshall *and designed the uniform for the new post himself. By the time of this photo the attempts to train a Filipino army had met with little success. MacArthur was working with the United States on plans to unleash devastating air attacks from the Philippines on Japan in the event of war.* (MacArthur Memorial Archives)

planes, tanks, and antiaircraft guns and the most advanced bombers available, long-range B-17s. They were called flying fortresses because of the machine guns they carried. Large formations of these planes could beat off fighter planes and deliver huge bomb loads deep inside enemy territories.

On November 15 Marshall summoned reporters from *Time, Newsweek,* and other publications and told them that all aspects of the Philippines buildup must remain secret. "The U.S. is on the brink of war with the Japanese," one of the reporters wrote in his notes of Marshall's comments. "Our position is highly favorable . . ."

Under great secrecy the U.S. is building up its strength in the Philippines to a far higher level than the Japanese imagine. General MacArthur is unloading ships at night, is building air fields in the closely guarded interior . . .

Most important point to remember is this: We are preparing for an offensive war against Japan, whereas the Japs believe we are preparing only to defend the Philippines . . . If it got out publicly the army fanatics in Japan would be in a position to demand war immediately, before we were better fortified . . .

If war with the Japanese does come, we'll fight mercilessly. Flying fortresses will be dispatched immediately to set the paper cities of Japan on fire. There won't be any hesitation about bombing civilians—it will be all out.

"Our aim is to blanket the whole area with air power," another reporter's notes quoted Marshall as saying. "Our own fleet, meanwhile, will remain out of range of Japanese air power at Hawaii."

Eventually, Marshall said, Japan would either back down or be quickly ravaged and eliminated as a serious adversary. Either way the United States would avoid a long Asian war and would be able to concentrate on Hitler, whose armies in November were closing in on Moscow. MacArthur expected Japan to attack in April 1942, and he hoped to be ready just in time.

In the first hours of December 8, 1941, Manila time, reports began to arrive of Japan's aircraft carrier attack on the U.S. forces at Pearl Harbor, Hawaii. At first the information was sketchy. MacArthur put his forces on alert and waited in the darkness. By then he had received just 35 of the 250 B-17s Marshall had wanted to send him. He'd ordered the planes flown 500 miles south to the islands of Mindanao—beyond the reach of Japan's bombers on Taiwan. But his air commander held 18 of the B-17s at Clark Field, near Manila, and tried to get permission for an attack on Taiwan.

As dawn broke these and a number of fighter planes took off and remained in the air to patrol and to avoid being caught on the ground. But at midday nearly all the planes landed to refuel and for the crews to have lunch. Shortly after noon Japanese bombers found the B-17s lined up in neat rows at Clark Field and destroyed them all. Here and at other airfields MacArthur also lost most of his 72 advanced fighter planes.

In a few hours Japan had all but eliminated the chances of the United States launching an effective bomber attack on an invasion fleet at sea or even contesting control of the skies over the islands. Most of the fleet that might have interfered with an invasion lay in ruins at Pearl Harbor. MacArthur's heavy shore guns had arrived from the United States but were not yet in place. He had just a few torpedo boats. Most of the 100,000 troops he had on Luzon had only the most basic training. Their weapons were few and antiquated. More planes, guns, ammunition, and equipment lay in the holds of cargo ships then steaming across the Pacific or at the docks in California. About 22,500 officers and men—many of them critically needed specialists in such areas as communications, artillery, and medicine—were also on their way or waiting to depart. But it was too late.

Wake Island and Guam, the U.S.-controlled stepping-stones west from Hawaii across the Pacific, came under Japanese attack within hours of the raid on Pearl Harbor and soon fell. British warships moving to disrupt the Japanese landings on the Malay Peninsula were quickly sunk by bombers, and soon the British were reeling back, down the peninsula toward Singapore. The United States quickly declared war on Japan, and Germany responded with a declaration of war against the United States. In the first week of the war Japan mounted five limited attacks in and around Luzon, mostly to secure airstrips. Planes pounded the U.S. air and navy bases, and a large Japanese invasion fleet closed on Luzon in the war's second week. MacArthur radioed frantically to Marshall. He urged that all available forces be mobilized to reopen supply lines and contest the enemy's air superiority. "If the western Pacific is to be saved it will have to be saved here and now," MacArthur declared.

Marshall answered that he was sending men and planes. Roosevelt promised publicly that the navy would bring "positive assistance to the defense of the Philippine Islands." But the small U.S. fleet based in Manila, with no air cover and its base wrecked, departed hastily to the south in late December. The Japanese landed in force on northern Luzon with little opposition. MacArthur's plan to fight at the water's edge turned to a shambles as inexperienced Filipino units folded and fled, losing stockpiles of food and ammunition.

The defenders regrouped and began a series of delaying actions against the Japanese units pushing south on Luzon. The general abruptly ordered his forces to evacuate Manila. His men scrambled frantically to move themselves and their supplies to Bataan, the mountainous peninsula at the mouth of Manila Bay, 10 to 15 miles wide and almost 30 miles long. Because MacArthur's defense plans had not allowed for this possibility the movement of supplies was bungled; the U.S. forces abandoned huge stockpiles of food in the rush to get to Bataan.

MacArthur moved his headquarters to the island fortress of Corregidor at the southern tip of the peninsula. The Quezons joined him and his family there. Under heavy bombing, they were largely confined in a system of cavernous tunnels, deep within the island rock of Corregidor.

As the Filipino-American forces withdrew into Bataan, they wrecked much of what American rule had accomplished. Railroads, docks, roads, bridges, pipelines, and telegraph cables were destroyed to deny them to the Japanese. Many of the poorly trained Filipino soldiers deserted. Others, especially the Scouts, fought furiously alongside the Americans against the new invader. On January 2 and 3 American and Filipino troops devastated Japanese units attacking near Bataan and kept the way open for their own units moving onto the peninsula.

Marshall radioed that long-range bombers were streaming across Africa toward British airfields on Malaya while other planes were "coming on every ship we can use." These, together with British reinforcements, he predicted, "should give us early superiority in the Southwestern Pacific." MacArthur, in turn, promised his men that Japan's control of the air would "soon be a thing of the past."

An army of about 85,000 completed the move into Bataan in early January, blowing up bridges as it withdrew. When the Japanese began to push south in pursuit, the Fil-American force, as it was called, inflicted heavy losses with artillery and drove them back. Scout and American gunners cunningly concealed their weapons in the jungle as Japanese spotter planes sought them out for targeting. Even when protective lines of infantry were swept away by waves of attacking Japanese, the gunners stood their ground and leveled the muzzles of their weapons to mow the enemy soldiers down.

While his soldiers fought, Quezon did all he could to secure an American commitment to save the islands. He secretly transferred $500,000 of Commonwealth funds—quite a fortune at the time—into a U.S. bank account of MacArthur's. Some of the money might have been due under MacArthur's ambiguously worded contract with the Commonwealth. But, this and smaller payments by Quezon to MacArthur's top staff were really gifts intended to strengthen the bond between MacArthur and those around him to the Philippine cause.

The payments remained a secret until years after MacArthur's death. He left no explanation for his acceptance of the money. In the Philippine culture it was fairly common for political figures to cement the loyalty of key supporters with payments. MacArthur undoubtedly was determined to expel the Japanese and preserve Quezon's Commonwealth government and the promise of its independence or to die trying. But men facing death for the same cause on Bataan got only the modest pay of soldiers.

In late January 1942, after more bloody fighting, the defenders withdrew to a new defense line about halfway down the peninsula. They fought on as lookouts anxiously scanned the horizon for signs of an approaching fleet or formations of American or British bombers. But help did not come. The British lost their Malayan airfields and retreated south to Singapore, where they surrendered February 15. Japanese planes ranged south from the Malay Peninsula attacking Allied airfields on Sumatra and Java, destroying many planes on the ground and cutting off air and ocean routes between British India and the Malay Archipelago. Marshall's promised buildup of air power never materialized.

MacArthur continued to bombard Washington with pleas for help. He even sent flattering messages to Stalin, believing that Russian entry into the war with Japan would shut down the invasion of the Malay Archipelago. "The hopes of civilization rest on the worthy banners of the courageous Russian army," the general radioed the communist dictator.

The Russians had pushed the Germans back from Moscow. But as Stalin fed troops by the millions into the inferno to his west, he had no interest in opening a second front to his east. The Japanese in turn ignored Hitler's pleas to attack Russia. Instead they settled into a stalemate in China and concentrated on taking Burma and on their massive campaign into the South Pacific.

Quezon fell into despair. He complained bitterly about Roosevelt's decision to concentrate on the defeat of Hitler. "America writhes in anguish at the fate of a distant cousin, Europe," he said, "while a daughter, the Philippines, is being raped in the back room."

He toured Bataan and wept over the young Filipino soldiers. "They are only being used to gain time on other fronts," he wrote in a memo to MacArthur, adding that their sacrifice would not help win the war. If the United States could or would not defend the islands it should grant them independence, he argued. The new nation would declare its neutrality and ask both Japan and the United States to withdraw their forces in order to "save [the] country from further devastation as the battleground of two great powers." Roosevelt rejected the idea, and soon Quezon and his wife left the island by submarine. They traveled to Australia and then on to the United States, where Quezon died before the war's end.

MacArthur sent a small trunk out by submarine with his will and pictures of his son. He pleaded with Jean to take the boy and go as well, but she refused. The general loaded an old two-barrel dueling pistol of his father's and swore the Japanese would never take him alive. "I intend to fight to complete destruction," he radioed to Washington. In return, the Japanese vowed to capture him and hang him in downtown Tokyo.

The tenacious resistance by Filipinos fighting under the American flag was an embarrassment to the Japanese. But this lone outpost of resistance did not slow the conquerors down. The two arms of the invasion reached from Taiwan through the Philippines and from Vietnam down the Malay Peninsula. Sumatra, Borneo, and Celebes fell easily. At the end of February the huge pincers of Japan's land, sea, and air forces closed on the opposite ends of Java.

There a ragtag fleet of mostly old Dutch, British, American, and Australian vessels made a futile show of resistance. On February 27 most of this force was destroyed off eastern Java.

In just 90 days, the Japanese had taken a huge empire. To the west they occupied Burma and cut the last direct route for aid from the Allies to China. To the south they secured Java and the other islands of the Malay Barrier and moved into western New Guinea. To the east their island conquests extended 2,000 miles into the Pacific. From one of their largest ocean bases, the port of Rabaul on what had been the English island of New Britain, Japan took footholds on the north coast of eastern New Guinea and in the Solomon Islands. Its bombers hit the small Australian garrison on the southern New Guinea coast, at Port Moresby, and raided into northern Australia itself.

Deep within this sea of Japanese power, an ominous calm settled over the battle front on Bataan. The attacking army, weakened by casualties and transfers of troops to other operations, pulled back to await reinforcements. MacArthur's besieged Fil-American soldiers used the lull to strengthen their positions, stringing barbed wire and communication lines, digging trenches and building gun emplacements.

But as supplies ran short, rations were cut. Filipinos and Americans grew feeble and sick within their bristling defenses. Marshall and one of his top generals, Dwight Eisenhower, continued frantic efforts to get supplies to the beleaguered army. A few small shipments made it in by submarine, but only one small surface vessel reached Corregidor. Numerous other ships were sunk, captured, or turned back. As Japan's navy and air patrols intensified, merchant captains would not try to run the blockade for any price.

Spurning Japanese demands for his surrender, MacArthur brooded in his underground headquarters. He visited the front so rarely that some of his embittered troops gave him the name of Dugout Doug. MacArthur was equally embittered toward Roosevelt and toward the leadership of the army and the navy, all of whom he believed had cynically misled, betrayed, and abandoned him and his men. He did not understand how desperately Marshall and Eisenhower had tried to get supplies to the Philippines and to build up enough air power to contest the Japanese. True, the failure of MacArthur's own air commander to safeguard his planes contributed to the general failure of allied air power. But it is also true that in the first weeks of the war Roosevelt's statements of support for the Philippines were stronger than the policy the president actually followed.

Years later MacArthur described how painful it was to witness the promise of democracy and independence in the Philippines vanishing in the shadow of another brutal conquest.

My heart ached as I saw my men slowly wasting away. Their clothes hung on them like tattered rags. Their bare feet stuck out in silent protest. Their long bedraggled hair framed gaunt bloodless faces. Their hoarse, wild laughter greeted the constant stream of obscene and ribald jokes issuing from their parched, dry throats. They cursed the enemy and in the same breath cursed and reviled the United States; they spat and jeered at the navy . . . [Filipino soldiers] would gather round and pat me on the back . . . They would grin—that ghastly skeleton-like grin of the dying—as they would roar in unison, "We are the battling bastards of Bataan—no papa, no mama, no Uncle Sam."

They asked no quarter and they gave none. They died hard—those savage men . . . like a wounded wolf at bay . . . And around their necks, as we buried them, would be a thread of dirty string with its dangling crucifix. They were filthy, and they were lousy, and they stank. And I loved them.

8

"THIS IS MY WAR"
March to September, 1942

As dusk fell over Manila Bay on March 11, 1942, the American torpedo boat PT-41 left the cove on Bataan where it had been concealed during the day. It motored south to the island fortress of Corregidor and pulled up to the bombed-out remains of a pier. A car arrived with Douglas MacArthur, his wife, Jean, his son, Arthur, and the child's Chinese nurse, Ah Chiu. The general, gaunt and pale, saw the other three aboard. He turned before climbing onto the boat himself and gazed back toward the island, a grim, rocky eminence rising steeply from the water. Bombs and shells had long since stripped its luxuriant vegetation away and shattered its buildings, leaving a landscape of blackened stone and rotting debris. "The smell of filth thickened the night air," MacArthur remembered years later. Red flashes of American artillery fire licked out from within the battered stronghold above.

He lifted his cap in a farewell gesture to the men who were watching him leave, and the muscles in MacArthur's face twitched uncontrollably. His defense of the Philippines was ending in failure. He had led 85,000 brave and loyal men to the brink of defeat and was about to leave them. To run from Corregidor was unthinkable, but President Roosevelt had repeatedly ordered him to leave.

The general's defiance of the Japanese had made him too much of an asset to faltering American morale to lose; for the

Douglas MacArthur's wife Jean, (right) and their son, Arthur IV, with the boy's nurse, Ah Chiu, shortly after the general and his family escaped from the Philippines to Australia in March of 1942 (MacArthur Memorial Archives)

Americans at Manila were not the only ones who felt surrounded. War wrapped around the world, from one side of the United States to the other. Americans counted the dead in the wreckage of Pearl Harbor; they saw the flames from merchant ships that the Germans torpedoed just off the Atlantic shore, and they picked up the sailors' bodies that drifted in to the beaches.

The United States and other powers formed a world alliance to combat the Axis powers (Germany, Italy, and Japan). But MacArthur's army was the only American ground force in the world during the early months of 1942 that was actually shooting at soldiers of an Axis power, and it was the only force of any country to hold out for long against the Japanese in the Malay Archipelago. Its ordeal of four months had been reported daily to the world by radio. Beaten or not, MacArthur was a heroic symbol of resistance. The Japanese wanted him dead. Roosevelt wanted him alive in Australia, to continue the war from there as commander of Allied forces in the southwest Pacific region.

MacArthur finally agreed to go. Having heard inaccurate reports of a massive American buildup in Australia, he imagined he would be able to lead a relief expedition back to the islands speedily. He turned command of the trapped army over to Jonathan M. Wainwright—the tough, lanky officer who had been the battlefield commander on Bataan. "Hold on till I come back for you," MacArthur told him.

The Japanese were on the alert. They knew MacArthur had become a popular figure in the United States and that some congressmen were calling on Roosevelt to bring him out. They controlled the sea and the air around Manila Bay for 1,000 miles or more. Nonetheless MacArthur decided against a relatively safe but slow escape by submarine. He climbed aboard the torpedo boat, and it motored slowly into the harbor, where it linked up with another three craft of the same type. Besides the MacArthurs, the total of 21 passengers included a dozen of the general's top staff officers.

Months of night patrol and raiding with inadequate maintenance had weakened the boats' engines. They could not manage to go above 25 miles per hour—barely more than half speed. The 77-foot craft rode low in the water. They were maneuverable, hard to spot between the waves, and hard to hit.

In the darkness they slipped past the enemy ships guarding the bay and turned south to travel down the east side of the Philippine Islands. Storms hid the moon behind clouds and raised 15-foot high waves. The boats pitched and pounded violently. Most of the passengers were soon soaked and seasick.

MacArthur lay retching on a mattress below deck while Jean, who was not ill, stroked his hands.

They reached the isolated Cuyo Islands at the north end of the Sulu Sea after dawn on March 12 and hid there. MacArthur decided to risk daylight travel that afternoon, and twice they barely missed detection by warships. After another tortuous night, the expedition reached the north coast of Mindanao the morning of March 13. It landed near a remote pineapple plantation whose airstrip and garrison of a few dozen U.S. troops had so far escaped the attention of the Japanese.

Two B-17s came in near midnight on March 16, picked up MacArthur's group, and took off for the 900-mile flight back to Darwin, Australia. They flew past Japanese air bases on the island of Timor as dawn broke, and they landed near Darwin on the north shore of Australia just ahead of an enemy air raid. The group hurriedly boarded a transport plane and continued south. Once beyond the reach of air attack MacArthur and his family boarded a train, as Roosevelt triumphantly announced news of the escape.

On reaching the city of Adelaide in southern Australia on March 21, MacArthur told reporters he had come for the purpose "of organizing the American offensive against Japan, a primary object of which is the relief of the Philippines. I came through and I shall return."

It was only after making this statement that MacArthur began to realize how difficult this journey would be. He soon learned that there were no more than 25,000 American troops in Australia. As for Australian soldiers, most of them had gone off to fight under British command in the Mediterranean region. The American troops were green—poorly organized and hastily trained. The air force was losing almost as many planes to accidents as to the enemy. Ships were indeed coming in with enough men to double troop strength, and with more equipment. But it would take months to create the complicated organization capable of meeting the Japanese in the jungles and in the air as well as on and beneath the sea. It was not clear when or where the Allies could check the enemy advance, let alone mount a drive to return to the Philippines.

"God have mercy on us!" MacArthur said on learning of the situation. His army at Manila was doomed and along with it all hope of avoiding a long war in the Pacific. He seethed over

Area Held by Japan, 1942

Extent of Japanese conquests

MacArthur's route, March 1942

0 — 1000 miles

0 — 1000 kilometers

In March 1942, Douglas MacArthur finally agreed to leave the Philippines. The escape was risky, but on March 21, he and 21 others safely reached Adelaide, Australia.

the failures of American leadership that he believed had led to this debacle.

Nevertheless, in public MacArthur professed to have faith in the Allied leaders. "I shall do my best. I shall keep the soldiers' faith," he vowed. Australian prime minister John Curtin and his government cabinet welcomed the general enthusiastically at the capital, Canberra. "I have come as a soldier in a great crusade of personal liberty as opposed to perpetual slavery," he told them. "My faith in our ultimate victory is invincible, and I bring you tonight the unbreakable spirit of the free man's military code . . . There can be no compromise. We shall win or we shall die."

So it was that, even as a fresh and heavily armed force closed in on Bataan's starving defenders, their shaken, inwardly seething and exhausted commander emerged from the disaster of Japan's conquests and declared the conquerors to be doomed. The audacity of his journey across Japanese-controlled sea and air space seized world attention. MacArthur, understanding that war had become something requiring the participation of virtually all an embattled country's population, used this moment to help mobilize opinion in the Allied countries in support of the war.

The Japanese and the Germans held celebrations as resistance on Bataan collapsed April 9 and Corregidor fell a month later. They ridiculed MacArthur, commander of the largest U.S. force ever to surrender to a foreign power. At least 20,000 Filipinos and Americans died in the last round of fighting and during a brutal death march that followed the fall of Bataan. Some of the survivors, left to toil and waste away in prison camps, cursed the general they thought had betrayed them, much as MacArthur privately cursed Roosevelt.

But millions of people hailed the escape from Bataan, as newspapers bannered the general's "I shall return" statement. In the weeks and months that followed babies and streets and buildings were named after MacArthur all over the United States. Roosevelt awarded him the highest decoration of the United States, the Congressional Medal of Honor, for having "confirmed the faith of the American people in their armed forces." The promise, "I shall do my best" led to a national campaign for people to sign copies of a statement promising that they, too, would "do my best" for the war effort. "This is my war," read the statement, which was topped with a picture of a saluting MacArthur. "Unless I do my best the war may be lost."

To MacArthur's outrage and dismay, the effort he helped to inspire did not focus on freeing the Philippines and knocking

Japan out of the war. Roosevelt faced pleas for troops and weapons from desperate Allied commanders around the world. He stuck to his promise to concentrate on the liberation of Europe and the defeat of Hitler. MacArthur saw this as militarily and morally indefensible. He thought that the Allies should dispose of Japan—the weaker of their enemies—first. He was sure that a massive thrust to the Philippines was not only the quickest and least costly way to shut down Japan's war machine and end the tragedy of the Pacific war; it was the sacred duty of the United States to liberate the people to whom the United States had been holding out the promise of freedom since 1898; it was their duty to free the soldiers who had been abandoned to fight without hope in order, as Roosevelt put it, to confirm "the faith of the American people in their armed forces."

The navy's top leaders, who chafed at being confined to a supporting role in the European war, joined MacArthur in support of a greater commitment to the Pacific; but they fought him for control over strategy and over the limited resources that were available. Roosevelt did not settle this army-navy conflict by putting a general or an admiral in charge of a unified Pacific command. Instead he divided the Pacific region. The southwest—including the larger land masses of Australia, New Guinea, and Malaysia—went to the army and MacArthur. The open ocean areas of the south and central Pacific went under the navy's command. The president ordered the two services to coordinate and to share troops, ships, and planes.

The Japanese drove on relentlessly to the south through the first half of 1942. But the vast area of their conquests had begun to stretch their forces thin. The Allies began to slow them down—with the help of a 1,500-mile natural barrier, New Guinea. This huge equatorial island stretches like a gigantic shield between the north Australian coast and the western Pacific ocean. It is rimmed by shallow seas and coral shoals. Its jagged 10,000-foot-high mountain spine, its coastal plains, deltas, and marshlands are soaked in tropical rains and swathed in jungles. Australia controlled the southeast coast of the island from the small trading center of Port Moresby. Japan occupied scattered outposts along the north coast. The opposing air forces attacked targets on land and sea and fought to control the skies from northern Australia to Rabaul.

In April MacArthur began to send a trickle of reinforcements to establish bases in the Moresby area and at Milne Bay, on the eastern tip of the island. The navy, meanwhile, rushed to build up strength in the islands of the New Hebrides, 1,500 miles east of Australia, and prepared to move north from there to meet the Japanese in the Solomons.

In early May Japan mobilized warships and troop transports for an attack on Port Moresby. But in the battle of the Coral Sea off the eastern coast of New Guinea, U.S. aircraft carriers thwarted the invasion. The following month Japan launched a massive naval force for another attack in the Hawaiian Islands, planning to destroy the Americans' three remaining carriers and thus to establish naval supremacy throughout the Pacific. But the weaker American force, which had the advantage of having broken Japan's communications codes, sank all four carriers in the attacking fleet, killing hundreds of Japan's best pilots.

The Japanese redoubled efforts to push MacArthur's forces out of New Guinea and to isolate Australia. In July a fleet from Rabaul landed 15,000 troops at Buna on the north coast of eastern New Guinea, directly across the island from Port Moresby. At first MacArthur refused to believe that the Japanese would dare strike directly south at Moresby. But they did, trying to move and sustain a force of thousands across tortuous trails through the jungles and mountains. By late August the general was rushing Australian and American troops to the defense of Moresby and Milne Bay. He appealed for transport ships and aircraft carrier support but could get none. The navy's move into the Solomon Islands had triggered a furious counterattack at Guadalcanal. Night attacks in the area by Japan's ships sank numerous American vessels and isolated the embattled U.S. marines on the island.

But at Guadalcanal and in New Guinea the Allies finally stopped the southward thrust of the Japanese Empire. The bloody struggle on Guadalcanal dragged on for months; but the Americans held on to the island. The Allies crushed the attack at Milne Bay in two bitter weeks. The attack on Port Moresby collapsed in early September—just 20 miles from its target, amid horrible scenes of starving, wounded, and diseased Japanese.

A brutal retreat began. Japanese officers shot their own wounded and diseased men rather than leave them to be captured alive. They left suicide squads behind to ambush pursuing Allied soldiers. Troops were forbidden to surrender, no matter what their situation. By killing as many of their

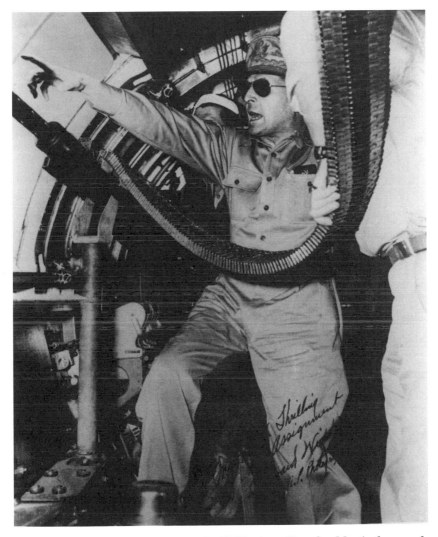

During his campaign to return to the Philippines, Douglas MacArthur made innovative use of air power to destroy enemy shipping, move large forces to attack enemy weak points from distant bases, and to support those forces with air-dropped supplies and equipment. In this photo the general rides in a bomber during an attack in New Guinea in 1943. (MacArthur Memorial Archives)

enemy as they could, regardless of the cost to themselves, some Japanese leaders hoped that the Americans would tire of the war. From Buna to Rabaul and throughout the captured territories in the Pacific islands, New Guinea and the Malay Archipelago, the Japanese prepared to defend their empire.

The first of their enemies to take the offensive was the last one they had beaten, Douglas MacArthur.

"RALLY TO ME"
1942–1945

As George Kenney listened to the tirade he noticed that Douglas MacArthur, even while in a rage, seemed to be watching him intently. "His eyes were keen," Kenney recalled, "and you sensed that wise old brain of his was working all the time."

Pacing his office in downtown Brisbane, Australia, Mac-Arthur studied his new air commander and described in scathing terms the outfit Kenney had just arrived to take over. Its officers were weak leaders and were obstinate toward him to the point of disloyalty, MacArthur complained, and its staff was incompetent and its bomber pilots ineffective. He was still livid over the recent Japanese landing at Buna. American and Australian pilots of the combined Allied air force had failed to do significant damage as enemy ships unloaded weapons, supplies, and men. In the aftermath MacArthur fired his air commander.

Kenney, a World War I fighter pilot who went on to become a general in the army air corps, was summoned immediately to fill the job. He was a stocky, good-natured man and a determined and resourceful fighter as well. He was the first of several aggressive combat commanders that MacArthur turned to in 1942 who helped to build a flexible and potent combination of land, sea, and air power.

Kenney did not try to address his new boss's complaints at their first meeting. He pledged his loyalty to MacArthur and quickly left to inspect air bases in Australia and New Guinea. He found that his fliers and ground crews in New Guinea could not even get netting for protection from malaria-bearing mosquitos that swarmed around their sleeping quarters. Nor could they get the spare parts needed to keep their planes flying. Of the 62 long-range B-17 bombers in his force a mere six were ready for combat.

"There were plenty of supplies and spare parts to put aircraft back in shape," Kenney wrote, "but these supplies and parts were in the southern part of Australia, two or three thousand miles from the war, and the [army] Supply Service boys down there didn't seem too concerned about sending the stuff forward. They figured the Japs would run us out of New Guinea, anyhow, and then the supplies would be properly located for the war in Australia itself."

When he got back to Brisbane Kenney promised his commander dominance of the air over the eastern New Guinea battleground; MacArthur gave him a free hand. When he took command in early August 1942, Kenney immediately began to shake things up. The effective air strength of the Allies jumped, and so did Japan's air losses. Bomber raids against Rabaul intensified, crippling Japan's efforts to keep the pressure on at Guadalcanal.

As the skies between Australia and New Guinea grew safer, another use of air power helped tip the scales in favor of the Allies. With MacArthur desperately short of shipping to move men and equipment from Australia to the island battle zones of New Guinea, planes began to do the job on a scale few people had believed possible. Kenney did not have many aircraft suitable for ferrying troops, but he transported thousands of men with passenger planes borrowed from Australian airlines. The army's heaviest trucks were too big to fit into cargo planes, so welders cut the truck frames in half and welded the vehicles back together upon arrival in New Guinea. Kenney also converted some of his more numerous small bombers into low-flying machine-gun platforms that preyed on the small supply and patrol boats of the enemy.

By making innovative use of whatever equipment was available and by building the morale of the military and of civilians, the American and Australian Allies put forth a tremendous war effort. Australia's Labor Party government, with the support of the country's workforce, brought about a rapid increase in production. Civilian workers put in untold hours of emergency overtime. Australia contributed food and many other basic supplies to both the Pacific and the global war efforts. MacArthur coordinated the export of Australian goods around the world to other countries fighting the Axis powers. In return he obtained factory equipment the Australians used to produce even more.

Thanks to this burgeoning war effort the Allies, who were barely able to hold on at Port Moresby in August and September, went over to the offensive in October. As the Japanese pulled into strongholds along the coast in the Buna area, the Americans and Australians prepared to attack. The navy would not risk any but the smallest ships in the shallow waters along the northern New Guinea coast, which were within easy reach of enemy planes at Rabaul. That ruled out an assault by sea. So MacArthur ordered the same type of arduous operation against Buna as the Japanese had tried on Port Moresby— moving men, guns, and supplies across the forbidding mountains and jungles of the island. But, unlike the Japanese, the Allies' superiority in the air allowed them to sustain their army partly with transport planes.

MacArthur, much of his headquarters staff, and even some of his field commanders did not really understand the conditions they were sending soldiers to face in the jungle. Columns of Australians and Americans moved through the mountains and approached the enemy strongholds in and around Buna. Resistance was generally light; but heat, insects, and sickness tormented the men. As they closed on the coast they found themselves in a web of rivers, marshes, and spits of land, with strong Japanese defenses on the dry ground. Fighting furiously, the defenders pinned the Allies in the swamps. Bad weather and enemy air attacks defeated efforts to tow barges of supplies up the coast from Milne Bay, and food ran short. Hungry, ill, disorganized, and miserable, the inexperienced American troops wilted. Their commanders said they needed more equipment to attack.

After weeks of stalemate, MacArthur grew desperate late in November. He feared that the Japanese would be able to land reinforcements at night, as they had repeatedly at Guadalcanal, and turn the offensive into an Allied disaster. From the forward headquarters at Port Moresby he summoned Robert L. Eichelberger, a commander who had been training American troops in Australia. "He was an angry and harassed man" when they met, Eichelberger recalled. MacArthur put him in charge of American forces at the battlefront and bluntly ordered him to take Buna or die trying.

"When you arrive up in this jungle," Eichelberger wrote to a friend in Australia a few days later, "you will find rising up in front of you, to haunt you, the spectre of all those things you have failed to teach your men." He urged that soldiers down to the level of corporal be trained in combat leadership because frontline officers died so quickly in the jungle. After failing to take ground in bloody frontal assaults, Eichelberger began learning from his enemy. His men advanced quietly at night and dug in, or climbed trees.

In the midst of the heaviest fighting MacArthur announced to the world that the worst was over. Except for some isolated pockets of Japanese, the eastern end of New Guinea was secure, he told the press. The general returned to Australia on January 8 1943, two weeks before the Allies finally crushed the Japanese at Buna. MacArthur hailed the first liberation of territory from the yoke of Japan. Having ordered Eichelberger to take Buna at all costs, he described the fighting as relatively easy, the casualties as light. In fact, about one in four of the 33,000 Allied troops in the campaign was wounded; more than 3,000 of them died—about half of the casualties came after the general declared victory.

MacArthur's press censors cleared news accounts of this fighting that were essentially fiction. Not only did they misrepresent the fighting, they described the general as being personally on the scene at Buna, though he had never crossed the mountains from Port Moresby.

Why would such a proud leader, trained from childhood never to lie and sworn as a soldier to uphold truth and honor, allow this to happen? In January 1943 MacArthur knew that Japanese strength was fading at Guadalcanal. The premature announcement of victory at Buna was well-timed to call attention to his own success. The lie about his presence at Buna could only have been intended to enhance his prestige. MacArthur cherished his heroic public image as the only weapon he had that could counteract the administration's bias in favor of Europe and the navy's attempts to force him into a minor role in the Pacific.

He clearly felt that incompetence and indifference on his own side of the war were as much of a threat as the Japanese. "It has been," as he confided to a friend in 1943, "a desperate time for me ever since the war started—always the underdog, and always fighting with destruction just around the corner. I could have held Bataan if I had not been so completely deserted . . . I am sick at heart at the mistakes and lost opportunities that are so prevalent."

While he was feeding the country news of victory that it longed for, he believed that the Roosevelt administration and the nation's military leaders would not want to be seen as holding back a popular and aggressive general. MacArthur's image became, in his mind, as sacred as his mission to free the Philippines. Kenney, who loved and deeply admired him, was amazed at the lengths to which the general's staff would go to get favorable press. Kenney wrote:

> His public relations officers invariably adored Mac-Arthur almost to the point of idolatry. To them unless a news release painted the General with a halo and seated him on the highest pedestal in the universe, it should be killed. No news except favorable news, reflecting complete credit on infallible MacArthur, had much chance of getting by the censors. They seemed to believe that they had a sacred mission, which was to "sell" the General to the world . . .

Public image became so important that MacArthur also considered it essential to squelch any notoriety that might overshadow his own—such as that of his talented battlefield commander at Buna. After a magazine article about Eichelberger appeared in the United States, MacArthur threatened to strip him of rank and send him home. MacArthur's willingness to depart from the truth, as well as his tendency to isolate himself at the center of a hard-working, adoring, and submissive staff, eventually twisted his ability to perceive the truth as well.

During the rest of 1943 the Allies moved painfully up the Solomon Islands toward Rabaul and westward from Buna along the New Guinea coast into the Huon Peninsula. MacArthur agreed with navy leaders that they had to secure these areas and take Rabaul or Japan would be in a position to disrupt the Allied offensive and regain the initiative.

The Japanese continued their fierce resistance. As at Buna and Guadalcanal, most of their soldiers fought to the death rather than surrender. But the Allies began to cope better with Japanese tactics and with the jungle. Quinine helped contain the ravages of malaria, and vitamins helped soldiers endure the heat and stress. In early March Kenney's planes caught a large Japanese flotilla bringing reinforcements to the Huon area, and not a ship nor hardly a man survived.

MacArthur was delighted with Kenney, who became one of the few newcomers to join his circle of trusted officers and—what was even more unusual—a close friend. Unlike ship and troop commanders who were based hundreds of miles away from MacArthur with their units, Kenney commanded his far-flung air force from MacArthur's headquarters in downtown Brisbane, on Australia's east coast. MacArthur was so fond of his blunt-spoken and effective air commander that Kenney was practically the only person who regularly breezed by the general's protective staff, walked unannounced into his boss's office, and made himself at home.

The Brisbane headquarters was a busy place. A dozen key aides and various staffs under them worked feverishly to decipher and analyze intercepted radio communications, aerial photographs, reports of snooping submarines and scout planes, spies and other sources of information about the Japanese. They planned complex operations involving land, sea, and air forces and requiring elaborate preparation of troops and supplies. They administered training and the constant flow of assignments, reassignments, and promotions. And they managed the enormous effort in providing fuel, transportation, ammunition, weapons, parts, equipment, and food to the army.

MacArthur began to get more ships from the navy, particularly flat-bottomed craft for landing troops and tanks on beaches. He used the term *triphibious warfare* to describe the complicated movements of troops over land, on transport ships, and by parachute to envelop enemy positions. He was consumed by the challenge of finding ways to use the new technologies of war to destroy his enemy without losing his own soldiers. Kenney, in an interview after his retirement, said he had never known another general who so valued the lives of his men:

"MacArthur would get the casualty list at the end of every twenty-four-hour period, and the tears would roll down his cheeks if one man was killed. Time after time he knew the guy, or he was the son of an old sergeant who had been with him someplace, or he was a lieutenant he knew when he was a cadet and MacArthur was boss at West Point."

Roger O. Egeberg, a doctor stationed in New Guinea, was another rare outsider who moved into the center of MacArthur's circle. He became the headquarters staff doctor and MacArthur's personal aide in 1943. Once, Egeberg said in an interview, "I asked him if he would visit some hospitals where we had the wounded . . . He said, 'No Doc, I feel responsible for every man in that hospital. They're all under my command, I feel that everyone [who] is sick, dying or badly wounded is mine. I can't do it, don't ask me.' And he said it almost pleadingly, and then he said, 'But take Jean. She'd like it and they'd probably like her better than me . . .'" MacArthur never got sick and would never allow Egeberg to give him a medical examination.

As the navy advanced north and west through the Solomons, the war at sea crossed into MacArthur's southwest Pacific combat zone, and the naval strength under the general increased. In April 1943 Admiral William F. Halsey, came to see his new commander at Brisbane. "Five minutes after I reported, I felt as if we were lifelong friends," Halsey recalled.

> We had arguments, but they always ended pleasantly. Not once did he, my superior officer, ever force his decisions on me. On the few occasions when I disagreed with him, I told him so, and we discussed the issue until one of us changed his mind. My mental picture poses him against the background of these discussions; he is pacing his office, almost wearing a groove between his large, bare desk and the portrait of George Washington that faced it; his corncob pipe is in his hand (I rarely saw him smoke it); and he is making his points in a diction I have never heard surpassed."

The tempo of operations picked up during the second half of 1943. In August, as the Allies were just approaching the Huon area, Kenney used another innovative tactic to destroy a large force of Japanese planes, about 400 miles farther west on the coast. He dropped teams into the remote jungle within range of his target, and they hacked out a small landing strip. Light planes flew in with more men and equipment, and the strip grew to accommodate larger planes. Within days Kenney had built an advance air base undetected under the noses of the Japanese. His fliers attacked with devastating surprise, destroying 175 planes on the ground.

The weakening of enemy air strength simplified the movement of men and supplies by ship in fighting that began the next month on the Huon Peninsula. In October massive air strikes hit Rabaul. By year's end the Allies had moved another 200 miles westward along the coast.

Early in 1944 MacArthur saw and seized a chance to complete the isolation of Rabaul and get on with his offensive. Bomber crews that had been hitting Japanese air bases in the Admiralty Islands, about 400 miles northeast of Rabaul, reported that all enemy planes had been withdrawn or destroyed. In just a few days MacArthur's commanders put together a task force that gained a foothold in the islands February 29. With allied planes based there, in the northern Solomons, and on the Huon Peninsula, Rabaul was surrounded by a ring of air power that cut off supplies and reinforcements and destroyed its port and airfields.

This cleared the way for an offensive westward and brought to a head a long-simmering dispute between MacArthur and the navy. The general believed that the long coast and huge land area of New Guinea would allow the rapid construction of air bases to give cover to the advance of sea and land forces, which could bypass most enemy strongholds and move quickly to the west. He adopted the tactic used around Rabaul of establishing air supremacy to cut off concentrations of enemy troops from supplies and transportation and leave them behind to "wither on the vine," rather than risk his own troops in direct attacks. After advancing the length of New Guinea MacArthur planned to jump north to the island of Morotai and from there into the Philippines. There, he argued, air power would strangle the flow of oil and other vital products and cripple the enemy decisively before a final confrontation at the home islands of Japan.

For a time it looked as if MacArthur's offensive would be limited to New Guinea while the navy went ahead with its own plan. The navy also favored an approach to the area of the Philippines. It began in late 1943 to move through Micronesia, the band of small islands lying north of the equator, including the Marshall Islands and Guam. To secure airstrips and ports in these islands troops had to go up against heavily fortified positions. The small land areas involved allowed little room for maneuver. Dramatic surprise attacks like those Kenney launched from secretly built jungle airstrips in New Guinea were out of the question. But the navy's route was about 1,000 miles closer to Japan than New Guinea was and would bring Japan within reach of the newest American long-range bomber, the B-29, sooner. The British and Americans had developed the idea of strategic warfare—fire-bombing of cities to destroy factories, housing, workers, and civilian morale—in the war with Germany. It was yet another way of using air power and, according to its advocates, could save time and lives on the Allied side.

Army and navy leaders in Washington eventually went along with both routes of attack. As before, MacArthur and his navy counterpart in the Pacific, Admiral Chester W. Nimitz, were ordered to coordinate and share resources. Attacking along two or more routes instead of just one is not an unusual tactic in the history of war. Two columns of forces moving in parallel give each other some protection and the possibility of reinforcement by one if the other gets into trouble. But the unusual scheme of sending two forces against the same foe without a common commander made coordination at best a clumsy and delicate process. MacArthur and Nimitz each thought of the other's campaign as unnecessary.

By early 1944 the initiative in the war had clearly passed to the Allies around the world. Eisenhower went to England as Allied commander in western Europe to make preparations for a landing of British and American troops at Normandy, France, and at last open a major new front in the war on Germany. The Russians pushed on into eastern Europe, while British and Indian soldiers fought the Japanese in the jungles of Burma.

Late in April 1944 MacArthur assembled a task force of more than 200 ships and 80,000 men. Bypassing nearly 500 miles of the New Guinea coast under Japanese control, the troops landed in the area of Hollandia, in Dutch New Guinea. Some of the fighting was very difficult, but more landings followed farther to the west in May. By the end of July the Allies had established themselves on the Vogelkop Peninsula at the eastern end of the island. It had taken more than a year, from October 1942 until the end of 1943, to secure the west end of New Guinea as far as the Huon Peninsula, a distance of about 400 miles. It took but seven months in 1944 for the Allies to cover almost three times that distance.

At the Admiralty Islands attack and many of the landings that followed, MacArthur went ashore not far behind the first wave of troops. He was in the habit of blithely striding forward "to get the feel of things" in areas under fire, with his nervous aides around him. He "stood up at the front when our men were lying on their bellies shooting, and he did all sorts of things like that," Egeberg recalled in an interview. MacArthur's amazing luck held.

In June and July the navy took Guam, Saipan, and Tinian in the Marianas Islands of Micronesia. Japanese carriers went after the U.S. fleet but lost nearly all of their pilots and planes. Soon the first B-29 raids began on Japan. That June the success of the D-Day Allied invasion of Normandy freed up war and transport ships for the Pacific. On September 15, 1944, as Eisenhower's army in Europe approached the Rhine Valley and the western border of Germany itself, the two columns of Allied Pacific forces began to converge on the Philippines. MacArthur's troops landed on Morotai to the south as Nimitz attacked the Palau Islands to the east. Leaving the Australians behind to cope with pockets of bypassed Japanese, MacArthur and the Americans pressed on.

On October 20, 1944, MacArthur returned to the Philippines with an invasion fleet of more than 700 ships and 200,000 troops. Halsey, who was back under Nimitz's command, maneuvered off the coast with more than 100 ships, including 18 aircraft carriers. At dawn the armada bombarded the eastern coast of the island of Leyte. The first assault wave of about 80,000 men hit the beach later that morning and quickly secured three beachheads. More men, equipment, and supplies poured ashore as MacArthur watched from the bridge of a cruiser.

Early that afternoon MacArthur went ashore with Sergio Osmena, who had replaced Quezon as president of the exiled Commonwealth government. The sight of burning landing craft, hit by mortar fire, and the sounds of sniper fire greeted them as they waded through knee-deep water to the beach. A portable transmitter was brought ashore, which beamed a signal back to MacArthur's cruiser, which in turn transmitted it throughout the islands. He spoke into a microphone: "People of the Philippines, I have returned! . . . Rally to me!"

Japanese reinforcements rushed to the island from Luzon. Thousands of men hurled themselves at the American lines and died under machine-gun fire. Some of the guns fired for hours on end, mowing soldiers down almost continuously, as

American troops land on the island of Morotai in September of 1944. One of more than 100 landings under MacArthur's command during the war in the South Pacific, this attack set the stage for an American invasion of the island of Leyte the following month, about 600 miles away in the Philippines. (MacArthur Memorial Archives)

the gun crews poured water on the barrels to keep them from melting. The battlefields, where thousands of dead and wounded men lay, in the tropical heat, became hideous, reeking scenes.

The last of the Japanese navy went after the invasion force and was destroyed, although at one point several enemy warships threatened the beachhead. Japanese fighters ranged over Leyte as MacArthur moved ashore and set up headquarters. As usual, he paid no attention to his safety. He had an air raid dugout at his house filled in because "it spoils the look of the lawn." One day an enemy fighter riddled the house with bullets as he was shaving, and he calmly continued stroking the razor along his face as if nothing were happening.

American carrier-based planes steadily wore down Japanese air strength. But a new tactic, suicide attacks by kamikaze pilots who would fly their planes right into ships, damaged numerous ships and killed hundreds of sailors. Landings on Leyte continued, and the Americans gradually isolated the island and pushed the remaining Japanese into the mountains, where fighting continued until May 1945.

At the end of 1944 the Americans landed on Mindoro, next to Luzon. On January 9, 1945, they landed on northern Luzon, where the Japanese had come ashore three years before. The Japanese gradually fell back into mountains in the northern part of the island, just north of Bataan and east of Manila. Some of them held out until the last days of the war. Some 30,000 Japanese naval troops holed up in Manila and trapped tens of thousands of Filipinos there.

MacArthur's forces reached the outskirts of the city in early February 1945. He refused to allow bombing of the city because of the trapped civilians. But many were caught in the cross fire between the opposing fighters, and some of the Japanese, in a frenzy, committed atrocities. Before it was liberated in early March, much of Manila was destroyed by artillery, and an estimated 100,000 civilians perished there.

Thousands of Filipinos, including many imprisoned by the Japanese, welcomed MacArthur joyously. When he reached the camps where the soldiers he had left in 1942 had been held, most were barely able to stand and whisper their thanks. Some looked on him with bitterness, not gratitude.

Douglas MacArthur, at the war's end in August of 1945, stands on a balcony in Manila, overlooking the ruins of the city. (MacArthur Memorial Archives)

On February 27, with Japanese resistance fading in Manila, MacArthur drove through the ruins of the city to Malacanan Palace, which had suffered little damage. In an emotional ceremony, he formally restored the Commonwealth government under Osmena. "Your capital city," he told the president and his hastily reconstituted cabinet, "cruelly punished though it be, has regained its rightful place—the citadel of democracy in the East. Your indomitable . . ." Arthur MacArthur II was speaking this phrase, "indomitable courage," when he collapsed and died in 1912. Douglas, already overwhelmed by the destruction of Manila, choked on the words. He stammered a request for the Filipinos to join him in the Lord's Prayer. "To others," he wrote years later, "it might have seemed my moment of victory and monumental personal acclaim, but to me it seemed only the culmination of a panorama of physical and spiritual disaster. It had killed something inside me to see my men die."

10

THE EMPEROR'S OVERLORD
1945–1949

Douglas MacArthur leaned back and dozed in the cabin of his airliner as it flew him into the arms of the enemy. On approaching Tokyo he woke and briefly admired Mount Fuji, then drifted back to sleep as the plane descended. An advance guard of fewer than 1,000 lightly armed American soldiers awaited him at Atsugi Airfield, where until recently kamikaze pilots had taken off on their suicide missions. Hundreds of thousands of Japanese troops and millions of civilians waited in the surrounding countryside, and in the ruins of their cities.

It was August 30, 1945—16 days after Emperor Hirohito announced Japan's capitulation and MacArthur was appointed to the most powerful position he ever held, the supreme commander of Allied forces in the Pacific. The general flew from the Philippines to Japan with his top headquarters staff and several field commanders to accept the surrender and oversee the occupation of the defeated country. He avoided a show of force, even ordering his nervous officers to take off their pistol belts.

The plane rolled to a stop on Atsugi's patched-up runway. MacArthur emerged and paused on the steps, as waiting photographers recorded the historic moment of his arrival. Then he and his officers set out in a motorcade of assorted cars for Yokohama, the port city just south of Tokyo, which MacArthur

Tokyo at the end of World War II (MacArthur Memorial Archives)

had visited with his parents 40 years before. Tens of thousands of Japanese soldiers lined both sides of the 15-mile route—their backs to the road, their rifles at the ready if need be to protect the new ruler of Japan.

Franklin Roosevelt began to steer this position to MacArthur early in 1945, as Germany collapsed and the Allied war effort focused more on the Pacific. After the fall of Manila at the end of February, Americans under Admiral Chester Nimitz attacked the fortified island strongholds of the Japanese at Iwo Jima and Okinawa. In weeks of heartbreaking combat, Nimitz seized the islands and brought Japan within easy reach of American air power. Under intensified bombing, the cities of Japan went up in flames.

The concept of strategic warfare—the destruction of an enemy's centers of production and population from the air—had been developed by the Germans and their British and American enemies during the war in Europe. With their armies separated by the English Channel, both sides tried various approaches to air war. The British and Americans learned how to destroy whole cities by firebombing. With a combination of high explosives and incendiary bombs, it was possible to create an inferno so powerful that it sucked debris into the fire from all directions, until there was practically nothing left. Several German cities were leveled in this way, with losses into the tens of thousands of people among the civilian populations. Allied officers explained to bomber crews that they were attacking civilians in order to destroy the enemy's ability to produce weapons and willingness to continue fighting.

The concept of breaking the will of an enemy power by wreaking havoc in the heart of its territory was nothing new; nor was it unprecedented to attack helpless noncombatants. But the development of the ability to hurl fireballs at cities from many hundreds of miles away represented a radical and historic change. The very idea of a limited battle zone, of the "front lines," began to disappear. Riding on the wings of the long-range bomber, the fire of war could reach almost anywhere, any time.

This was the war that came to Japan starting in late 1944. Except for a few religious centers of little importance to the war effort, the country's cities were devastated. Hundreds of thousands of the inhabitants died. But the American army's planners still expected the Japanese to fight to the very end in their home islands, just as they had fought everywhere else. So the Allies prepared to follow up the bombing with a massive invasion to bring the war finally to a close. Roosevelt, just before he died in office that April, designated MacArthur to lead the invasion and occupation of the enemy's homeland. Harry S. Truman, thrust suddenly into the presidency, stood by his predecessor's decision.

In the months after Manila fell in February 1945, MacArthur concentrated on liberating the rest of the Philippine Islands. He also took two ports on Borneo from the bypassed Japanese garrisons on that island. By the middle of the year MacArthur was able to declare all the Philippines liberated. As he prepared for the invasion of Japan the general began to predict privately that it might not be necessary. The air war was so devastating, Kenney wrote, that the Japanese were showing signs of collapse and willingness to surrender. According to Kenney, he and MacArthur learned of plans for the use of a devastating new type of bomb, and both men thought it was not needed. On a trip to Washington, however, Kenney found that the top army officers there did not share his view that Japan was almost ready to give up.

On August 6 the city of Hiroshima disappeared beneath the fireball of an atomic bomb, followed three days later by Nagasaki. The power of this new weapon was comparable to that of the firestorms created with ordinary bombs. But with the atomic bomb mass destruction came from a single plane, rather than waves of bombers; it was instant and total. The age of strategic war had just dawned when it moved into a realm of virtually unlimited power and destruction.

As he rode into Yokohama on August 30 after the emperor announced Japan's capitulation, MacArthur saw a ghostly landscape of charred rubble where a city had stood. More than three-quarters of the buildings had been destroyed by firebombing. Most of the surviving inhabitants had fled to the countryside. The general and his staff temporarily took over one of the few undamaged buildings remaining, a hotel. To the north, the ruins of Tokyo lay under the guns of a huge allied fleet.

MacArthur addressed the Japanese people and the people of the world from the deck of the *Missouri* on that historic September 2, 1945, the day that World War II ended. He used this moment to warn that humanity could no longer endure the consequences of unlimited war between great powers.

"A new era is upon us," MacArthur declared. The amazing growth in the power of weapons "has in fact now reached a point which revises the traditional concept of war." He turned to the occupation of Japan knowing full well the price the victors in World War I had paid for their failure to establish a durable peace. That disastrous war was but a prelude to the even greater disaster of World War II; and now another failure to secure peace could lead to destruction on a truly catastrophic scale.

The bombers that leveled Tokyo had avoided hitting Emperor Hirohito's palace. An office building nearby that had also escaped serious damage became MacArthur's headquarters. He and his family moved into the U.S. embassy, which had suffered only light damage. Amid the rubble of Japan's capital city, MacArthur's plan for building peace unfolded.

Many Americans—and even more Asians who had suffered under the Japanese empire—expected to see a harsh occupation, one designed both to punish Japan and to stunt its economy so that it could not again become a major power. But MacArthur set out to help the Japanese rebuild their shattered country. Having seen how the collapse of democracy during the 1930s led to the rise of warlike dictatorships in both Japan and Germany, he embraced the mission his father had described, to "plant firmly and deeply the best type of republican institutions." Democracy rather than retribution, MacArthur had

Emperor Hirohito of Japan visits his country's new ruler, Douglas MacArthur, at the American embassy in Tokyo in September of 1945. (MacArthur Memorial Archives)

concluded, was the foundation of peace. "The human impulses which generated the will to war, no less than the material sinews of war," he wrote, "must be destroyed."

To build democracy in Japan MacArthur planned a series of sweeping constitutional, political, economic, and social reforms. They were not to be imposed at gunpoint by a conquering army but rather implemented by the Japanese themselves and incorporated permanently into the society. The country, MacArthur later wrote "had become the world's great laboratory for an experiment in the liberation of a people from totalitarian military rule and for the liberalization of government from within."

MacArthur immediately followed up his conciliatory words at the surrender with millions of tons of food, which his troops doled out to a nearly starved population. Late in September newspapers throughout Japan published a picture of the emperor and the general together during a visit by Hirohito to the embassy. This was a signal from the emperor, whom the people had traditionally worshiped as a divine ruler, for the Japanese not only to submit to occupation but to accept MacArthur's leadership.

The Japanese accepted stoically two glaring departures by MacArthur from his posture of restraint and his "cherished wish for freedom, tolerance and justice." In what American critics charged was nothing less than judicial murder, MacArthur orchestrated the trials and executions of two Japanese generals who had fought him in the Philippines.

Masaharu Homma, who led the army that conquered Luzon in 1941, was charged on flimsy evidence with responsibility for the death march that followed the fall of Bataan. Tomoyuki Yamashita, who commanded Japan's unsuccessful defense of the Philippines in 1944 and 1945, was tried for the atrocities committed by Japanese naval troops in Manila—even though these troops had acted against his explicit orders. Whatever MacArthur's motives—personal revenge or a desire to give some satisfaction to the outraged Filipinos—the trials were a mockery of American standards for relevant evidence and impartial judgment. But they drew little notice in the United States.

Nor did the Japanese pay much attention to the fates of Yamashita or Homma. The people were disillusioned with their military and relieved that the Americans punished a limited number of people without adopting a vindictive attitude toward the entire population. As the Japanese labored at the lengthy task of rebuilding their country physically, a political and social transformation began.

MacArthur ordered the Japanese to disarm their own troops. Within a few weeks of the ceremony on the *Missouri* millions of soldiers, including many returned from China and other parts of the vanquished empire, had turned in their guns and uniforms. Japan no longer had an army. The secret police were disbanded and political prisoners released. Within a few months a new constitution, based largely on a proposal drafted by MacArthur and his staff, was adopted.

The constitution established a parliamentary democracy. The emperor, who voluntarily renounced the idea that he was divine, became only a symbol of national unity. The constitution abolished the concept of nobility; it guaranteed freedom of speech and religion, recognized full citizenship and voting rights for women, the right of workers to organize unions and the right of citizens to organize political parties. Responding to letters that poured into his headquarters from Japanese citizens, MacArthur explained that not only could women vote, they could run for and hold office.

The constitution drew on the experience of democratic states around the world. But one of its provisions was unique. It read:

> Aspiring sincerely to an international peace based on justice and order, the Japanese people forever renounce war as a sovereign right of the nation and the threat or use of force as a means of settling international disputes . . . Land, sea and air forces, as well as other war potential, will never be maintained. The right of belligerency of the State will not be recognized.

Some historians have suggested that MacArthur wrote this provision. He claimed for the rest of his life that it had come from the Japanese themselves. Their prime minister, Kijuro Shidehara, proposed it, according to MacArthur's account, so that "the old military party would be deprived of any instrument through which they could someday seize power, and the rest of the world would know that Japan never intended to wage war again . . . Whatever resources the nation had left should go to bolstering the economy."

This language brought ridicule in Japan and elsewhere—especially from "cynics who said that it was against the basic nature of man," MacArthur wrote. He insisted that the no-war provision did not void Japan's basic right of self-defense. But, in renouncing the right to make war beyond its shores, he said, Japan was the first country in the world to embrace a concept that might someday win universal acceptance.

The constitution, including the no-war clause, was adopted by the Diet, Japan's legislature, in March of 1946. The next month saw a large turnout for the election of a new legislature. Women took 38 of 466 seats. The Diet followed up on the general constitutional reforms with new laws guaranteeing specific rights. For example, it revised marriage and divorce laws that had made wives virtually the property of their husbands.

Having replaced a semifeudal state with a democracy, MacArthur and the new government moved on to attempt major changes in the society itself. They broke up the business conglomerates that had dominated war industries and other parts of the economy and also attacked concentration of land ownership. In his approach to economic reform MacArthur tried to build on the American Jeffersonian tradition of democracy, based on a belief in the right of ordinary people to own property and have economic independence. MacArthur's greatest success was in land reform.

Unlike the feeble land distribution program that the general had sponsored in the Philippines, the effort he led in Japan was massive and had lasting impact. Beginning in 1947, absentee landowners were forced to sell their properties to the government at low prices. The government in turn sold land to small farmers on affordable terms. Within a few years the overwhelming majority of families tilling the soil for a living owned the land they worked.

Some of the initiatives taken by Japan under MacArthur had limited or only temporary impact. He tried to loosen centralized control over schools and textbooks, but this did not last. In the 1990s Japanese scholars are still fighting the suppression of history texts that deal honestly with the story of brutality and exploitation in Japan's Asian empire and in the war. The concentration of economc power among a few huge conglomerates having close ties to the government has become a fact of life in late 20th-century Japan. Yet political power is spread across a broad spectrum of groups. There is a large and politically strong labor movement and also a large and powerful class of peasant landowners.

The country has established a small "self-defense" force and has even begun to make its own jet fighters. Many of its leaders refuse to acknowledge Japan's role in starting World War II or the murders, massacres, and grotesque human experiments committed by its army on hundreds of thousands of defenseless people. Nor, in the eyes of its victims, has Japan faced up to the oppression of millions or the abduction into sexual slavery of thousands of Asian women for the army's use.

But, more than half a century after the end of the war, Japan is one of the top three economic powers in the world and yet is still militarily insignificant. Though there is a right wing in Japan that romanticizes the days of empire, leaders who voice understanding and remorse for the empire's crimes have become increasingly assertive. A book of reminiscences by Japanese from all walks of life (*Japan at War: An Oral History*) reveals agonizing memories of brutality and of boys and young men used as cannon fodder by the empire's war machine. Polls show that an overwhelming majority of the people support the no-war clause of the constitution.

Douglas MacArthur was not the only American leader who believed in an occupation policy of reconstruction rather than retribution. Most of the initiatives he undertook were the official policy of the U.S. government under Harry Truman. But the speed and the extent of reform in the first years after the war were largely the result of MacArthur's influence and ability. Clearly he was a founding father of the modern Japan.

The Japanese revered him. Crowds gathered daily at the headquarters building just to watch the general arrive for work in the morning or to see him return from lunch at the embassy in the afternoon. He maintained the image of a distant but compassionate sovereign, much as the country's emperors had done. Thousands of people wrote letters to him. He read all of this mail, with the help of a translator, and responded to each letter. His routine varied little. Most days, including weekends, he worked into the night. He did not tend to mingle or socialize, and he traveled very little either in or outside of Japan.

MacArthur presided as a remote ruler over a staff of thousands of American military and civilian specialists. The overwhelming majority of them saw him very rarely or never. A core of a dozen trusted aides and department heads controlled the flow of reports and recommendations to his desk. This headquarters establishment supervised virtually every activity of the Japanese government, from vaccination of the population against disease to reconstruction of cities and train systems to the operation of courts. But for all that the general accomplished with his organization, it catered to his ambition and at critical times it blinded him.

Back in 1942, Dwight Eisenhower referred disdainfully in his diary to MacArthur's inner circle of aides as "his bootlickers." They were, as a rule, extremely hard working and loyal; but unlike him they were not combat leaders or colorful personalities. Kenney, Halsey, Egeberg, and other relatively strong friends and associates moved on in the first years after the war. During the late 1940s no one in Tokyo dealt with MacArthur on anything approaching equal terms. By his own choice, he did not have people around him who were comfortable questioning major decisions or even pointing out embarrassing facts.

MacArthur himself compounded this weakness of his staff with his own arrogance and sense of infallibility. "He considered himself a man of destiny, and above others," Eisenhower said in 1965, after having spent eight years as president of the United States himself. Philip LaFollette, one of the general's adoring press aides during World War II, later remembered MacArthur as an "almost perfect combination of human qualities," including dazzling brilliance and superhuman will. His one serious flaw was a lack of humility, LaFollette wrote. "He could never laugh at himself—never admit mistakes or defeats. When these occurred they were never admitted, and he resorted to tricks—sometimes sly, childlike attempts—to cover up."

For example, in 1948 MacArthur used the story that he was not really a candidate for president of the United States to cover up the crushing disappointment of being an early loser in the race for the Republican nomination.

MacArthur undoubtedly believed that he could and should become president. As Truman's standing in public opinion polls dropped through 1947 it began to look as if the Republicans would at last end a 16-year Democratic hold on the White House. With encouragement directly from the general, his supporters set up MacArthur committees in the early primary states—especially in his family home of Wisconsin. Many of the more conservative and anticommunist Republicans there and across the country, including the Hearst newspaper syndicate, favored MacArthur. Wisconsin was also home to the staunchly liberal populist, Philip LaFollette—who later became governor of the state. LaFollette, who, despite MacArthur's conservatism, saw the general as a gifted champion of freedom and human rights, went all-out for his old boss.

Many of the old isolationist Republicans opposed MacArthur. Another candidate, Harold Stassen, had the support of Wisconsin's junior U.S. senator, Joseph McCarthy, who dug up all of the general's marriage and divorce records. Just before the primary date, in April 1948, the senator spread the records before voters—under the guise of questioning whether MacArthur was a Wisconsin resident but actually to suggest that there was something embarrassing about his personal life. McCarthy argued that MacArthur was out of touch with civilian problems and too old to "undergo the strain of years as President of our country at this difficult time." Other claims about MacArthur's sexuality and mental stability circulated by word of mouth.

The general trailed far behind Stassen in the Wisconsin voting. A few weeks later, after another disappointing showing in South Dakota, he withdrew from the primaries. That June the Republicans nominated Thomas E. Dewey, who went on to fall before a surprise Truman surge in the November election.

Whether he still hoped for a chance at the presidency or not, MacArthur followed American politics and world events closely and continued to cultivate a hero's image in news coverage of his administration in Japan. But he paid little attention to some of his own responsibilities in areas outside the public spotlight. He ignored the Philippines, which achieved independence in 1946 but where U.S. forces remained under his command. And, while he strove to root freedom and democracy deeply in Japanese life, he made no similar effort for millions of Japan's victims nearby on the Asian mainland who, after decades of oppression, had been placed under his protection.

11

A NIGHTMARE OF FOLLY
The Korean Crisis
1950–1951

When the Soviet Union's armies overran the Asian territories of Imperial Japan in the last days of World War II, Joseph Stalin's troops occupied most of Manchuria, in northern China. Then they joined with the Americans to free the 50 million people of Korea, who had suffered under the heel of Japan for 40 years. The Soviets moved into the northern half of the 600-mile-long Korean Peninsula. The Americans landed in the south. The two powers agreed to use the 38th Parallel (which crosses the peninsula at its narrow midsection) as a temporary boundary between their forces until a new world organization, the United Nations, could hold elections for a Korean government.

But Korea did not have national elections, nor did it achieve national unity. The Soviets sponsored formation of a communist regime in the north. The American commander in the south, General John R. Hodge, received no guidance from his boss, Douglas MacArthur, on how to administer southern Korea. Desperately short of soldiers, Hodge employed Korean police and administrators who had worked for the hated Japanese. This only exacerbated the polarization of the country into two hostile camps, one in the north under the Soviets and one in the south under flimsy American protection.

Hodge's troops and police crushed a rebellion by desperate South Korean peasants and workers in 1946. From Tokyo, MacArthur wrote that he was unfamiliar with the Korean situation and could offer no advice. In exasperation Hodge requested transfer out of the country; MacArthur responded that he should take a vacation and "forget about Korea" for a while.

Indeed, as global competition developed between the United States and its former Soviet ally in the years after the war, U.S. leaders concluded in 1947 that they could forget about Korea. They drew the boundary of what came to be known as the Free World across the western Pacific off the shore of Asia, from the Aleutian Islands in the north to Japan and on to the Philippines in the south. In 1948 both the United States and the Soviet Union began to withdraw their forces from Korea,

August, 1950: A wounded American soldier is evacuated as U.S. and South Korean troops, under attack by North Korea, retreat to the southern tip of the country. (International News Photo)

with each one leaving a government behind in the zone it had occupied. Each of the rival regimes vowed to destroy the other and reunify the country.

The hostility between the world's two greatest powers, the United States and the Soviet Union, was intense almost from the end of the war. But at first the competition was more economic and political than military. The Americans rushed to rebuild Western Europe so that economic hardship would not turn people toward communism, and to build a barrier in that continent against the spread of Soviet influence. Secure in the knowledge that the United States had the world's only stockpile of atomic bombs, the Truman administration relied on this advantage to keep the Soviets in line. Truman quickly reduced army, air, and naval forces after the war and continued to cut them through the late 1940s as he struggled to balance the budget and support economic programs in the United States and Europe.

The American sense of security suffered two major shocks in 1949. In August the United States detected an atomic test explosion by the Soviets—at least two or three years before anybody in the United States dreamed that they would have the capability. Two months later communist Chinese armies under the command of Mao Zedong routed the forces of nationalist warlord Chiang Kai-shek. As Chiang fled to the island of Taiwan 100 miles off the China coast, taking with him all his soldiers, Mao proclaimed from the national capital of Peking (Beijing) the creation of a communist Chinese people's republic.

These two events helped to drive to new heights of frenzy the anticommunist hysteria that had been growing in the United States since the end of the war. After the bombing of Hiroshima and Nagasaki Russia's dictator, Joseph Stalin, had launched an all-out espionage effort to steal atomic secrets from the British and Americans. The U.S. politicians, led by Wisconsin senator Joseph McCarthy, charged that, not only had American communist traitors given the bomb to the Russians, but that they were part of a sweeping conspiracy to destroy the United States. Reds, McCarthy and his allies declared, had infiltrated the U.S. government itself and the state governments, in addition to major institutions such as the universities, the schools, the entertainment industry, and the labor movement. In the McCarthy view of things this sinister conspiracy had already caused the U.S. government to abandon Chiang and hand China over to Mao. McCarthy and other congressmen unleashed a campaign to drive communists, suspected communists, and communist sympathizers out of American life. MacArthur was openly sympathetic toward this crusade and also took steps to suppress communism in Japan.

Truman went along with this. But still, he saw no need for an all-out arms race. He did accelerate production of atomic bombs and ordered a crash program for development of an even more destructive weapon, the hydrogen bomb. But, while striving to maintain overwhelming superiority in the weapons of strategic war, he continued to cut the total military budget. Nor did Truman and his advisers—unlike McCarthy and his group—equate Mao's triumph with the formation of a Chinese-Soviet communist bloc. The administration figured that it would be able to exploit conflict and mistrust between China and the Soviet Union and keep them from joining forces. So, notwithstanding angry denunciation from anticommunist leaders, Truman refused to risk provoking Mao by sending troops or supplies to Chiang.

By the end of 1950 all this had changed drastically. A fabulously expensive global race had begun, with the development and production of all kinds of weapons and with the raising of massive, permanent armed forces. The world powers and numerous smaller allies divided up into two opposing blocs. They spent the next four decades preparing for a third world war and trying to contain and outmaneuver one another in poor countries around the world. This became the third great military confrontation of the century, the cold war. It was triggered in part by vacillating American policy in Korea and by Douglas MacArthur.

Leaders in the administration and Congress and even the general himself had all said in published interviews that Korea was not vital to U.S. security. But they were taken by surprise when North Korean troops and tanks advanced across the 38th parallel and headed south in June 1950. The South Korean army, its American advisers had reported, was the best in Asia and could handle the North Korean forces with ease. Instead, South Korean resistance collapsed.

The Truman administration and the top military leaders of the United States, the Joint Chiefs of Staff, interpreted this as part of a global communist strategy of aggression. Though Korea itself had been considered unimportant, the American leaders concluded that it was essential to "contain" communism and not to "appease" Stalin the way Europeans had appeased Hitler before World War II. So Truman reversed American policy and won United Nations endorsement of what he called a limited "police action" in Korea, to be conducted by the United States and its allies, particularly Great Britain and Turkey. He ordered MacArthur to intervene immediately with U.S. troops from Japan in order to "hold" South Korea.

Reports from MacArthur's own staff failed to reveal just how unprepared the American occupation forces in Japan were for combat. Hurriedly MacArthur shipped his ill-trained soldiers to Korea and flung them into the teeth of a much stronger North Korean force. Thousands of Americans were killed. The rest retreated in confusion. MacArthur stripped Japan of troops, and the Truman administration sent more reinforcements, until the American forces in Korea totaled nearly one quarter of a million. In desperate fighting during July 1950, U.S. troops and 60,000 South Koreans managed to establish a defensive perimeter around the port of Pusan in southeast Korea. This was a tiny area about 50 miles square.

From the outset MacArthur made decisions beyond his authority as a military commander. He sent troops to Korea and took other steps—such as air attacks on North Korea—after he had asked his superiors in Washington for permission but before they granted it. One officer at the general's Tokyo headquarters recalled, "MacArthur put into effect what he asked for before he got permission, to my personal knowledge, including the introduction of the first [American ground forces] into Korea . . . He went ahead and did what he asked for, and each time it was approved [afterwards]. An amazing experience!"

As he had in the past, MacArthur issued statements catering to his image at home as a great fighter against tyranny. He infuriated Truman and helped to convince the Chinese that the Americans intended to overthrow their government by publicly advocating an alliance with Chiang. The administration and many military leaders suspected that the Soviets were preparing to attack Europe and that they had ordered the North Korean invasion as a diversion. While the American leaders viewed Korea as a limited war in a global confrontation, Mac-Arthur flatly declared that the fate of the free world was at stake in Korea. He did everything he could to undermine the administration's policy of waging a limited war.

As the North Koreans spent their strength in bloody attacks against the Pusan perimeter in August, the general demanded and finally won permission from the Joint Chiefs of Staff in Washington to send a force by sea to attempt a difficult landing at Inchon, a port city on the west coast of the peninsula, near the South Korean capital of Seoul. This force would liberate the capital and strike across the peninsula to trap the North Korean army to the south. "We will land at Inchon and I will crush them," MacArthur said.

For reasons that are not easy to fathom, MacArthur named his chief of staff, General Edward M. Almond, to lead the invasion force. Almond, who had earned MacArthur's favor as an energetic administrator, had little combat experience. He was arrogant, abusive, and had a relationship with the Pusan commander, Walton H. Walker, that verged on mutual hatred. In mid-September, as MacArthur watched from a navy battle cruiser, Almond landed with 100,000 army troops and marines at Inchon. From his air-conditioned headquarters on shore, where he enjoyed hot showers and dined on fresh food flown in daily by the air force, Almond demanded that his soldiers take Seoul by September 25, the date by which he had promised MacArthur the city would fall. Obsessed with producing a "liberation" on schedule that left Seoul in ruins, Almond did nothing to prevent most of the North Korean army from retreating northward up the peninsula and making good its escape.

Success at Inchon caused delight in Washington and another change in policy. The United States and its allies, Truman decided, would not stop at their previously declared goal of preserving South Korea. Instead their forces would pursue the North Korean forces across the 38th parallel, destroy them and reunite the country. Communism would not only be repulsed but rolled back.

The Chinese were already concerned about U.S. navy ships patrolling the waters between the mainland and Taiwan and about Chiang's obvious eagerness to draw the United States further into the Korean conflict. Mao had seen the Japanese

Douglas MacArthur met with President Harry Truman on Wake Island, in the Pacific, in mid-October of 1950, after an offensive by the United States and its allies drove the North Koreans from South Korea. Together, they were largely responsible for the decision to attack into North Korea, toward the Chinese border. (MacArthur Memorial Archives)

invade China from Korea 20 years before, in 1931. He put the word out publicly and through diplomatic channels that China would not allow the Americans to occupy North Korea. Neither Truman nor MacArthur showed concern. Before launching the full-scale invasion of the north, the two men flew to remote Wake Island in mid-October to meet. If the Chinese tried to come in, MacArthur assured the president, "there would be the greatest slaughter" inflicted from the air. The Central Intelligence Agency (CIA) told Truman that China probably would not intervene.

Even while Truman and MacArthur were talking at Wake Island, tens of thousands of Chinese soldiers were marching secretly into the mountains of North Korea. They had no trucks, tanks, artillery, or other heavy equipment. They moved on foot by night and hid by day.

Moving up across the 38th parallel, Walker's force captured the North Korean capital of Pyongyang. Almond's force boarded ships at Inchon, sailed around the peninsula, and landed on the east coast above the 38th parallel. In the Pyongyang area the peninsula is less than 150 miles wide. But to the north it grows much wider until, in the area of the border with China and Russia, Korea measures more than 400 miles across.

MacArthur now brought his military career to a close in a nightmare of folly. The general, who complained so bitterly about the divided command of American Pacific forces in World War II, divided his forces between the two independent field commanders while he remained in Tokyo, hundreds of miles away. His two forces were physically isolated from each other by rough terrain, so they could not coordinate or keep the enemy from moving between them and attacking them separately. MacArthur ignored orders from the Joint Chiefs of Staff to keep well away from the Yalu River, whose winding course marks the Korea-China border. He launched his rival commanders on a mad race to see which of them could get to the Yalu first. The farther they moved northward into Korea's vast border region the more separated the American forces became.

Starting in late October 1950 the Chinese began their intervention with a series of relatively limited attacks on American and allied forces that were pressing into the northernmost provinces of North Korea. The Chinese attacked by night in great masses of troops, engulfing and wiping out opposing units. Again defying instructions from his superiors, MacArthur ordered an all-out bombing campaign to level every city and village in the border area and to knock out bridges across the Yalu River. He believed that air power would allow him to isolate and defeat the Chinese and North Korean forces south of the Yalu.

The joint chiefs, who had tamely submitted to MacArthur's orders for an American advance to the Yalu, canceled the general's bombing campaign. "Men and materiel in large force are pouring across all bridges over the Yalu," a furious MacArthur wrote in a message cabled back to the chiefs. He demanded that the dispute be "immediately brought to the attention of the President as I believe your instructions [canceling the bombing] may well result in a calamity of major proportions for which I cannot accept the responsibility."

President Truman received this message on the eve of elections in which his party's control of Congress was at stake. Facing what looked like a threat by MacArthur to resign while accusing him in effect of helping the Red Chinese kill American soldiers, Truman backed down. MacArthur got his bombing campaign. It was devastating, but it did not impede the Chinese soldiers. They used pontoon bridges in place of bridges the bombers had destroyed. As the bitter cold winter closed in, the Chinese troops simply walked into Korea across the frozen Yalu. They moved by night. They were not detected, much less slaughtered, from the air. The Americans did not realize that a huge force was closing in.

Mao's army, commanded by Marshall Peng Dehuai, pulled back from the battered Americans north of Pyongyang at the beginning of November. Some of the more moderate leaders in Beijing thought that the attacks might persuade the Americans to reconsider their plan to occupy North Korea and instead to withdraw back to the 38th parallel. Peng's orders were to leave the Americans alone if they pulled out of the north; but if they did not leave North Korea or if they continued to push toward China's border Peng was to renew the offensive and drive them into the sea.

Peng waited for three weeks, all the while preparing his next attack and carefully reading news dispatches radioed from Korea and Japan to U.S. newspapers. On November 24 MacArthur put out a statement to the press saying not only that he would continue toward the Yalu but explaining in some detail how and when he would do it. The statement, which was in Peng's hands within hours, explained that Walker's and Almond's forces formed two separate "pincers" that were about to "close the vise" on the Chinese and North Korean forces and "for all practical purposes end the war" by unifying all of Korea. The statement also revealed to Peng MacArthur's illusory belief that air power had "successfully interdicted enemy lines of support from the north . . ."

MacArthur's intelligence officers, knowing what the general wanted to hear, slanted their reports to downplay the Chinese threat. Walker and Almond, even as they encountered ominous signs of the Chinese presence, did not dare question the soundness of the general's plans. Almond sent one of his detachments hundreds of miles ahead of his main force, all the way to the border of China, and dispersed his forces across northeast Korea.

The day after MacArthur's statement, Peng launched attacks by more than 300,000 troops. The attackers suffered horrendous casualties, but they routed the South Koreans and drove American, British, and Turkish forces back, trapping thousands of men in forward positions. Many died fighting heroically to keep paths of retreat open for their comrades; thousands did not make it back.

Almond's troops fought their way back to the east coast, where the guns of the *Missouri* and other battleships offered some protection at the port of Hungnam. From there Almond's force was evacuated, and he went back to a desk job in Tokyo. Walker's troops retreated toward the 38th parallel, as the Chinese streamed south after them.

On November 28, 1950, President Truman grimly accepted the conclusion of his advisers that the Chinese were acting on instructions from Joseph Stalin. He decided that the United States must limit the war in Korea and prepare quickly for general war with the Soviet Union. Truman agreed to ask Congress for a tripling of the military budget to pay for a massive program of rearmament and troop mobilization. A few days later he said publicly that the use of the atomic bomb was an option in Korea.

The Joint Chiefs of Staff wanted MacArthur to pull his troops into easily defended positions and to hold on while political leaders tried to get the Chinese to negotiate. But the general wanted to implement his own war policy, not Truman's. He demanded massive reinforcements and called for a blockade of the China coast and atomic bombing of Chinese bases in Manchuria. He also wanted to collaborate with Chiang in an attack from Taiwan against the Chinese mainland.

The general declared that by preventing him from attacking China the joint chiefs were imposing a crippling restriction "unprecedented in military history." He did not wonder why the Chinese were not striking at Japan with bombers and submarines they could obtain from Russia. In fact, believing that escalation of the war might lead to a nuclear confrontation between the United States and the Soviet Union, both sides exercised restraint outside Korea even as they created carnage on the peninsula.

MacArthur could not accept this policy of limited war. In his view war meant the use of all the power needed to win. Spending the lives of soldiers for the political purpose of "containment" of communism was unthinkable. Truman had adopted the goal of freeing and unifying Korea. When the president decided to abandon this objective in the face of China's massive intervention MacArthur did all he could to thwart this change in policy. He insisted that attacking China or pulling out of Korea were the only alternatives. At first the joint chiefs were not sure if he would accept their plans to hold on in South Korea. At one meeting General Matthew Ridgway, who was by then second in command of the army, was amazed that the chiefs would not order MacArthur to do what they wanted done. Finally, he wrote, "I blurted out—perhaps too bluntly but with deep feeling—that I felt we had already spent too damn much time on debate and that immediate action was needed. We owed it, I insisted, to the man in the field and to the God to whom we must answer for those men's lives to stop talking and to act. My only answer from the twenty men who sat around the wide table, and the twenty others who sat around the walls in the rear, was complete silence." The joint chiefs could not control their general and did not dare dismiss him. MacArthur was a national hero who had been in uniform longer and fought in more wars than any of them. He was, as Eisenhower had put it, "an untouchable." Even the president shied away from confronting him.

MacArthur, under gentle prodding from the chiefs, did order General Walker to set up a series of defense lines running across the peninsula and to fall back from one to the next as Chinese pressure built. But Walker died in a traffic accident in late December, and Ridgway was immediately appointed to replace him. A tough paratroop commander who had fought in Europe in World War II, Ridgway also had misgivings about the idea of limited war. But he accepted the duty of the military to implement the president's policy.

In early January 1951 the Americans retreated below Seoul. Ridgway worked feverishly to reorganize and revive his dispirited men. His strategy focused on inflicting casualties rather than holding territory. As MacArthur continued to send dire messages to Washington from Tokyo predicting the collapse of his forces, Ridgway counterattacked and actually pushed the

Chinese back. Seoul was recaptured once again, and the fighting dragged on, surging north, and then south up and down the narrow midsection of the peninsula. MacArthur, who had sworn that this could not happen, became irrelevant. The Joint Chiefs of Staff began quietly to bypass him, reports and instructions moving directly between them and Ridgway.

MacArthur seemed to pay no attention to the Truman administration's objectives or even to military common sense. Whenever Ridgway launched a major attack, MacArthur would fly in briefly to be on hand and make statements to the press. The Chinese soon learned that if their spies in Tokyo detected the general leaving Japan, an attack was on the way.

Late in March 1951 MacArthur learned that, with the military situation stabilized, Truman was about to try to open negotiations with the enemy to end the war. In a letter to a congressman, which he knew would be released, the general once again called for a wider war with China. "We must win," he wrote. "There is no substitute for victory." Then he released a statement suggesting that the United States and its allies might abandon their "tolerant effort to contain the war to the area of Korea through expansion of our military operations to [China's] coastal areas and interior bases." Having been instructed not to make policy statements, the commander of American and allied forces in the Pacific was publicly calling for all-out war with China. This, his statement warned, "would doom Red China to the risk of imminent military collapse." In light of these "facts," MacArthur wrote, he was ready to meet with the enemy commander to arrange "the realization of the political objectives" of the allies—namely the reunification of Korea under a noncommunist regime—"without further bloodshed."

With the president of the United States about to make an overture for negotiations, MacArthur upstaged him and threatened China with an attack on its own territory if it did not give up North Korea. Whatever the merits of his differences with Truman on policy might be, this action was beyond MacArthur's authority as a military commander and contrary to direct instructions from the president not to issue policy statements. It was a deliberate act of disloyalty not merely to Truman himself but to the presidency.

Truman, though he knew full well that it would not help his already fading hopes of winning another term in the White House, did not hesitate to act. He stripped MacArthur of all command authority and replaced him with General Ridgway. MacArthur professed to be surprised. As in World War II, he had tried to use his popularity in the United States to influence national policy and had used the prospect of his resignation or dismissal to pressure those who opposed him. Now, at the age of 70, this last confrontation focused attention on his opposition to a policy of limited war and put MacArthur in the spotlight of a controversy that dominated national attention.

As he rode to an airport near Tokyo the Japanese lined his route again, as they had when he arrived in 1945. But this time the people along the road, 250,000 of them, were grateful civilians rather than soldiers of a defeated army. As the general flew with his family back to the United States, millions heaped condemnation on Truman. MacArthur was hailed as a hero at a ticker tape parade in New York City and also in Washington, where he addressed a joint session of Congress. There he repeated his view that war was the greatest threat to humanity, that he prayed for it to end for all time. "But," he added, "once war is forced upon us, there is no other alternative than to apply every available means to bring it to a swift end." He was, he said, just doing his duty.

The acclaim he received triggered renewed interest among some Republicans in nominating MacArthur for president, but only briefly. The general testified at lengthy congressional hearings on the Korean War and embarked on a national speech-making tour. But the acclaim and attention faded, and the Republicans turned to another popular general, Eisenhower, to get the White House back at last.

MacArthur did not succeed in discrediting the idea of limited wars to contain global communist movement. The Korean War continued into 1953, as Truman and then Eisenhower pursued negotiations that brought not actual peace, but an armed truce. Korea remained on the front lines of the cold war until it was over. Even after the Berlin Wall came down and the Iron Curtain across Europe fell, Korea remained split along the 38th parallel into two bitterly hostile states.

Furthermore, Truman and the presidents who followed him extended the same containment policy that they pursued in

Korea to China's southern flank—the southeast Asian countries of Laos, Cambodia, and Vietnam. In the 1960s and 1970s this led to disaster for these peoples and also for the United States.

Amazingly, democracy blossomed south of the barbed wire and trenches that mark the divide between the two Koreas. The government the Americans sponsored was democratic in name but corrupt and tyrannical in fact. In spite of this the South Koreans themselves have asserted the right to freedom and self-government. Many South Koreans revere Douglas MacArthur as a defender of their country. But they cannot, as many in the Philippines and in Japan do, count Douglas MacArthur among the founders of their democracy.

EPILOGUE:
"LISTEN! O LISTEN!"
1951–1964

As he stood before the U.S. Congress to give his farewell speech in April 1951, Douglas MacArthur had the ears of the country and much of the world for the last time in his life. He ended with a melancholy line from an old barracks ballad: "Old soldiers never die. They just fade away."

"And like the soldier of that ballad," he said, "I now close my military career and just fade away—an old soldier who tried to do his duty as God gave him the light to see that duty."

But MacArthur's image did not fade readily from the American scene. Nor had he, even as an aging civilian, finished with what he considered his duty. He had time to think about his experience of war in the 20th century and to study the development of the cold war in the 1950s. He tried until the last days of his life to have the country and its leaders listen to his conclusions.

After a hectic year in which he defended his conduct of the Korean War before Congress and in speeches around the country, the general gave the keynote speech at the Republican convention that nominated Dwight Eisenhower for the presidency in 1952. Eisenhower won the election and took office early in 1953. For the next eight years Eisenhower virtually ignored his old boss. The president did not seek the general's advice on military matters, Asian policy, or anything else.

Douglas and Jean lived in quiet luxury with their son in an apartment at the Waldorf-Astoria in New York. Arthur IV showed no interest in a military career. Eventually he became a musician. Douglas became chairman of the board of the Remington-Rand corporation, a major defense contractor.

Politically MacArthur remained a conservative, rabidly opposed to heavy taxation, to government interference in the economy, and above all to communism. But in 1955 he became the only one of the American leaders who had helped initiate the cold war to publicly condemn its consequences. In a speech to a California chapter of the American Legion he called modern war "a Frankenstein . . . the darkest shadow which has engulfed mankind . . ." The "bald truth," he told the veterans, is "that the next great advance in the evolution of civilization cannot take place until war is abolished." This was so, the general argued, because war itself had become obsolete. The cold war had placed millions of people in the two blocs of opposing powers in the path of a holocaust. Year after year preparation on both sides for all-out war consumed hundreds of billions of dollars that if wisely spent "could conceivably abolish poverty from the face of the globe." Because each side matched advances in the weaponry of the other, the arms race would accomplish nothing, MacArthur declared.

> We are told we must go on indefinitely as at present—some say fifty years or more. With what at the end? None say—there is no definite objective. They but pass along to those that follow the search for a final solution. And, at the end, the problem will be exactly the same as that which we face now. Must we live for generations under the killing punishment of accelerating preparedness without an announced final purpose or, as an alternative, suicidal war . . .?
>
> [War] is no longer an ethical equation to be pondered solely by learned philosophers and ecclesiastics but a hard core one for the decision of the masses whose survival is the issue . . . When will some great figure in power have sufficient imagination and moral courage to translate this universal wish—which is rapidly becoming a universal necessity—into actuality?

MacArthur's speech attracted some notice. But in the White House his former aide continued the policies adopted by Truman, building a system of global containment around the Soviet Union and its allies that relied mainly on military rearmament and often on alliances with dictators in impoverished countries. Eisenhower believed in what he called the "domino theory" in Southeast Asia. If he allowed Vietnam to "fall" to communism—even if he allowed democratic elections, which he believed Vietnam's communists would win—this, he believed would inevitably cause neighboring countries to become communist one after another, like a line of falling dominoes; and the system of containment in Asia would collapse.

Thus, during the mid-1950s the cold war came to dominate the world. It had tremendous impact on the economy of the United States and, to an even greater extent, of the Soviet Union. Development of missiles, advanced aircraft, and ever more sophisticated "conventional" and nuclear weapons called an entirely new American arms industry into existence, whose design and production centers were scattered along the East and West Coasts and across the South. This industry generated high profits, high-paying jobs, and political clout. Like its counterpart in the Soviet Union, it became part of a huge defense establishment with a strong vested interest in the notion that the cold war and a war economy would go on indefinitely.

Soon after Eisenhower left the White House in early 1961, MacArthur's status there abruptly reached a level that was unprecedented since the Hoover administration. In April of that year the new president, John F. Kennedy, visited MacArthur in New York. Kennedy knew MacArthur by reputation as "a reactionary old soldier," according to a White House aide. Kennedy probably thought that seeing him would help blunt accusations that the administration was being "soft" on communist Cuba and its leader, Fidel Castro.

Kennedy was stunned by the advice he received from MacArthur and invited him to the White House several times to discuss his ideas in depth. According to Kennedy's aide, "MacArthur was extremely critical of the military advice that the President had been getting from the Pentagon . . . MacArthur implored the President to avoid a U.S. military build-up in Vietnam, or in any other part of the Asian mainland, because he felt that the domino theory was ridiculous in a nuclear age. MacArthur went on to point out that there were domestic problems—the urban crisis, the ghettos, the economy—that should have far more priority than Vietnam."

MacArthur undoubtedly believed that Kennedy might have "sufficient imagination and moral courage" to tackle the issue of war. Indeed, after securing ratification of a nuclear test ban treaty, the president repeatedly called attention in speeches to the cost of the arms race. He was, as recent research has shown, preparing to reverse his own policy of increasing U.S. involvement in Vietnam, though whether he actually would have done so will never be known. When Kennedy was assassinated in Dallas on November 22, 1963, MacArthur cabled his widow, "The world of civilization shares the poignancy of this monumental tragedy."

Early in 1964, even as his health failed, MacArthur continued his lifelong habit of avoiding doctors. In March, when it became clear that he was very ill, President Lyndon B. Johnson had him flown to Walter Reed Army Hospital in Washington and visited him there. As he had done with Kennedy, MacArthur urged Johnson to avoid involvement in Vietnam. Death spared MacArthur from seeing Johnson's decision, in the summer of 1964, to ignore this advice and to embark on a war policy in Southeast Asia.

Doctors operated three times, trying to save the general from intestinal problems and a failing liver and kidneys. He fell into a coma on April 3 and, with Jean by his side, died two days later at the age of 84.

From the banks of the Rio Grande in New Mexico to the 38th parallel in Korea, Douglas MacArthur's life followed the westward progress of American power. He was born as the last armed resistance of the American Indians flickered out under the overwhelming pressure of wealth, weapons, and numbers; he experienced the checking of American power by the Chinese in Korea at the end of his career; and he died warning against a second and even more disastrous attempt by the United States to influence the history of Asia through force of arms.

MacArthur's personal experience of war extends from the ascendancy of the machine gun early in this century to the atomic age. His story is one of vision and of blindness, of idealism and of cynicism. He is but one among many military leaders who have claimed to serve humanity. But he is rare among them in disputing the idea that war is a natural and inevitable part of human affairs and in calling for its total elimination.

It is hard to see how the ideas he offered in his last years could reflect anything but the best effort of a brilliant and disciplined mind to understand the truth and to conceive of and to seek a fundamentally different and much better world. At that point in his life there was no career, no ambition, and very little public attention to color his judgment; his arguments do not seem calculated to settle old scores or vindicate his own past.

Today, in the late 1990s, it seems that events since his death — particularly the course and the outcome of the Vietnam War — do vindicate much of what MacArthur said in his last years. And now, with the cold war receding into history, he should be remembered not just as a general but as a great student of human history, one who believed in the power of humanity to understand its past and to make its own future.

FURTHER READING

Nonfiction Books

Astor, Gerald. *Crisis in the Pacific: The Battles for the Philippine Islands by the Men Who Fought Them — an Oral History:* New York: Penguin, 1996.

Cook, Haruko Taya and Theodore F. *Japan at War: An Oral History.* New York: New Press, 1992.

James, D. Clayton. *The Years of MacArthur 1880–1941. Vol. II: 1941–1945. Vol. III: Triumph and Disaster, 1945–1964.* Boston: Houghton, 1970–1985.

James, D. Clayton with Anne Sharp Wells. *Refighting the Last War: Command and Crisis in Korea, 1950–1953* New York: Free Press, 1993.

Luvaas, Jay, ed., *Dear Miss Em: General Eichelberger's War in the Pacific, 1942–1945.* Westport, Conn.: Greenwood, 1994.

Rasor, Eugene L. *General Douglas MacArthur, 1880–1964, Historiography and Annotated Bibliography.* Westport, Conn. Greenwood, 1994.

Schultz, Duane. *The Last Battle Station: The Saga of the U.S.S. Houston.* New York: St. Martin's, 1985.

Whan, Vorin E. Jr., ed. *A Soldier Speaks: Public Papers and Speeches of General of the Army Douglas MacArthur.* New York: Praeger, 1965. Includes the full text of MacArthur's 1955 speech on war.

Fiction Books

Remarque, Erich Maria. *All Quiet on the Western Front.* Originally published 1929. Numerous editions are available

Documents

The most important collection of documents is at the MacArthur Memorial Archives in Norfolk, Virginia. The archives are extensive and very well organized, including MacArthur correspondence, photographs, microfilm, and photocopies of important documents from other collections, copies of the numerous interviews with MacArthur associates by biographer D. Clayton James and others, and an extensive library. I am greatly indebted to the archivist James W. Zobel for access to these materials. The MacArthur Memorial also has a museum with extensive exhibits on the general's life.

Published documents available at many libraries include:
82nd Congress, First Session. *Military Situation in the Far East: Hearings Before the Committee on Armed Services and the Committee on Foreign Relations, U.S. Senate.* Two Volumes. Washington: Government Printing Office, 1951. (The MacArthur hearings)

57th Congress, First Session. *Hearings on Affairs in the Philippines.* Senate Document 331, vol. 2. Washington, D.C., 1902. (For testimony of General Arthur MacArthur II, see pages 849–1968, especially 862–909.)

Asia and the South Pacific: Maps and Handbooks

Goodenough, Simon. *War Maps: World War II from September 1939 to August 1945: Air, Sea, and Land, Battle by Battle.* New York: St. Martin's, 1982.

Lye, Keith. *Asia and Australasia*: A brief introduction to the land, economy, culture, and people of Asia, Australasia and the Pacific Islands. New York: Gloucester, 1987.

Messenger, Charles. *World War Two: Chronological Atlas.* New York: Macmillan, 1989.

Ulack, Richard and Gyula Pauer. *Atlas of Southeast Asia.* New York: Macmillan, 1989.

Taylor, Robert H., ed. *Asia and the Pacific: Handbooks of the Modern World.* New York: Facts On File, 1991.

INDEX

Italic numbers indicate illustrations.